Praise for
Carefree Black Girls

"Blay's personal experiences with astute cultural analysis explore how joy has become one of the most useful weapons in a Black woman's arsenal."　—*Bitch Media*

"Blay's observations about the impact Black women have had and continue to have on pop culture are searing and timely, and will have a lasting impact on how much the world sees and understands us."
　　　　　—Tarana Burke, founder of the Me Too
　　　　　movement and author of *Unbound* and
　　　　　You Are Your Best Thing

"Blay is a talent, mixing an encyclopedic knowledge of pop culture, past and present, with incisive commentary on race and gender and the unsurpassed wit of Zora Neale Hurston. A passionate, beautiful writer, Blay leaves me cackling during her much-needed, under-heard sermons."
　　　　　—Janet Mock, *New York Times* bestselling author
　　　　　of *Redefining Realness* and *Surpassing Certainty*

"With the delicate, lifesaving skill of a surgeon, Zeba Blay delves into the body of white supremacist capitalist patriarchy to get to the heart of misogynoir. . . . Blay's idea of Black womanhood is an inclusive one, where liberation is not just possible, but doable because it has the space for all Black women—cisgender, transgender, rich, poor, old, young, local, global—magnifying the potential for unity (and success) against the forces which mean them harm. . . . Each essay carries with truths that feel ancestral. *Carefree Black Girls* is the testimony I've been waiting to witness."

—Robert Jones, Jr., author of *The Prophets*
and creator of Son of Baldwin

"Black women have been narrowly escaping demolition from the moment they dared to build themselves. Blay picks up the rubble from untold stories and shatters the cycle of silence by giving her improbable, 'inconvenient,' and incredible Black girl body a full voice. Blay tells her Black girl truth and in so doing doesn't simply reclaim the narrative but constructs an entirely new one on her own firm and fertile ground."

—Michaela Angela Davis, writer/image activist

CARE
FREE
BLACK
GIRLS

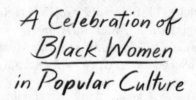

A Celebration of
Black Women
in Popular Culture

ZEBA BLAY

ST. MARTIN'S GRIFFIN
NEW YORK

Library of Congress Cataloging-in-Publication Data

Names: Blay, Zeba, author.
Title: Carefree black girls : a celebration of black women in popular culture / Zeba Blay.
Description: First edition. | New York : St. Martin's Griffin, 2021. | Includes bibliographical references. |
Identifiers: LCCN 2021016071 | ISBN 9781250231567 (trade paperback) | ISBN 9781250231574 (ebook)
Subjects: LCSH: African American women in popular culture. | Blay, Zeba. | African American women— Biography—Anecdotes. | African American women— Social conditions. | Sex in mass media.
Classification: LCC E185.86 .B58 2021 | DDC 305.48/896073—dc23
LC record available at https://lccn.loc.gov/2021016071

For little Zee

Contents

Author's Note

Many of the essays in this book reference mental illness, suicide, racial violence, transphobia, sexual abuse, disordered eating, body dysmorphia, and other traumatic barriers to freedom. I promise it's not all heavy, but if some of these themes are triggering or upsetting for you, please be tender with yourself as you continue.

CARE FREE BLACK GIRLS

Introduction

Abook called *Carefree Black Girls* could be about a lot of things, and so I want to start by giving you some sense of what this book is and what it is not. I wrote the bulk of these essays during the most difficult time in my life thus far. Between 2018 and 2020 (years that spanned the traumatic sea change of my Saturn Return), I felt as though I were in a never-ending emotional spiral, a constant falling. This feeling was only intensified by the fact that the world, too, was spiraling, a series of unfortunate events springing up one right after another: the morbid absurdity of the 45 presidency, the revelations of the #MeToo movement, the continued rise of the alt-right and neo-fascism and MAGA fanatics, livestreamed mass shootings, global protests against police brutality, the hell of the last U.S. presidential election and its aftermath, the wildfires in California and Australia, the widespread loss of life due to COVID-19, violent attacks against the Asian American community, black squares on Instagram, and the relentlessness of Black death.

While we were all collectively grappling with the existential dread brought on by these upheavals, several personal, world-burning occurrences happened to me in quick succession. I recovered long-repressed memories of sexual assault, some visceral, some hazily defined. I fell into the deepest state of depression and anxiety I have ever experienced in my life. I became a citizen of the United States after a period of living in precarity as an unwanted immigrant. I turned thirty. I attempted to take my own life, twice.

Prior to the suicide attempts, I had stopped regularly leaving my apartment for weeks that gradually turned into months on end. The longest stretch (in which I only ever ventured into my building's lobby to pick up fast-food delivery) was four months. This hermiting, mind you, began long before the days of COVID-19 and social distancing. In March 2020, when people were just starting to get used to the idea of working from home and avoiding strangers, I had already been consistently doing both for months. The virus merely heightened and validated my desire to hide, to burrow into my little corner of melancholy and anxiety and neuroses.

Not leaving my apartment had nothing to do with a

fear of the world. It had everything to do with a fear of being myself in the world. Facing depression and trauma, especially trauma that you have been avoiding for nearly a lifetime, forces you to question who you are and where you stand. What is real and what isn't? It's as though every cell in your body is changing and you are painfully transforming, bit by bit, into an entirely new human being. There's no room for dishonesty when you're going through that kind of transition. There's nowhere to hide. And so, being a person in the world felt like an impossibility, because in order to be "out" and be "on," I believed that I had to be dishonest, to pretend as though I was OK when I wasn't.

On the rare occasions when I did go into the office (where I worked full-time as a culture writer for *Huff-Post*), I felt like a robot with some sort of glitch. I felt defective. How could I do my morning commute, go to meetings, and make small talk with my colleagues when I could barely get out of bed? How could I answer even a mundane question like "how are you?" with "I'm fine," knowing that the real answer was "I haven't slept in seven days and I feel like I'm beginning to see things from the corner of my eye"?

Until I could say I was fine and truly mean it, leaving my apartment was too exposing. Instead, I did the thing I've always done when I try to cope with bad feelings—I wrapped myself up in the warm cocoon of my home and disappeared into movies, into TV shows, into the internet. I discovered and rediscovered things that made me feel warm and seen and safe. I rewatched old seasons of *Girlfriends* and *Moesha,* listened to albums like Erykah Badu's *Mama's Gun* and Junglepussy's *Satisfaction Guaranteed* and Minnie Riperton's *Perfect Angel* on repeat as a meditation, read Claudia Rankine and Octavia Butler and Saidiya Hartman and felt my heart catch in my throat. I watched, over and over again, a 30-second clip from a Nina Simone interview in which she declares, "I'll tell you what freedom is to me. No fear!" Slowly, bit by fragile bit, I wrote.

All this to say: the essays in this book came together as I fell apart. And writing about Black women is the thing that put me together again, that got me through, and helped me become reacquainted with the concept of joy and freedom.

I'm constantly, maybe even obsessively, thinking about what it means to be a Black woman who writes about pop culture. A Black woman who watches. I have been writing, mostly about film and television, for over ten years. In my work, in the conversations I have online and offline, there is a truth I always find myself coming back to: Black women are everything. To say that Black women are everything, that they are indeed a driving force if not *the* driving force of popular culture, is not intended as some pithy, abstracted, tweet-able declaration, a slogan to slap onto a t-shirt or a coffee mug. To say that Black women are everything, are indeed essential to American culture, to the global zeitgeist, is simply to observe things as they actually are.

Arguably the most celebrated and influential pop stars

within the last decade and the current one are two Black women: Beyoncé and Rihanna. Both have defined and then redefined what it means to reside at the intersection of business and artistry. Visual storytellers, including Ava DuVernay, Michaela Coel, Issa Rae, Mara Brock Akil, Misha Green, Dee Rees, Janet Mock, and Shonda Rhimes, have changed the film and television industries from the inside out by creating stories centered on Black characters who look, behave, and live lives radically different from anything that's been seen before.

On Instagram, baddies and models of every ethnicity rock fashion and beauty trends that Black women either created or popularized: cornrows, oversized door knocker earrings, long, intricately designed acrylic nails, artfully sculpted baby hairs. Other so-called beauty trends are imitations of the actual physical attributes of many Black women. People pay small fortunes for lips, asses, and melanated skin tones modeled after Black women (whether the people getting these treatments are conscious of it or not) to be carved, pumped, and injected into their non-Black bodies.

Yet the culture that Black women pour their talents and their creativity into, the culture that emulates Black women, steals from Black women, *needs* Black women, is the same culture that belittles Black women, excludes Black women, ignores Black women. One moment, Beyoncé is hailed as a pop cultural deity who can do no wrong (a kind of praise that leaves little room for her humanity or meaningful critique). Another moment, the internet debates whether her daughter Blue Ivy, a beautiful little Black girl, is ugly because she has inherited the features of her father, Jay-Z (wide nose, thick lips). Exploring that unreality, that state of being seen but unseen, essential but unacknowledged, loved but disrespected, is part of what this book is about.

In 2013, I was the first person to tweet #carefreeblackgirl, which eventually became a popular phrase used to celebrate Black women, much like #BlackGirlMagic and #flexinmycomplexion. The tweet was auto-posted from an Instagram post, a blurry picture of my then twenty-four-year-old self smiling in front of my alma mater, The New School, captioned with: *I go to school to give looks, then I leave. #carefreeblackgirl*

Only a few hours before I posted that tweet and that picture, I was fantasizing about suicide the way one would fantasize about a lover. This was several weeks after my birthday, which had put me in an implacable funk. I was experiencing that need to hide that often sets in when I'm sad, an uneasiness with being seen, heightened by feeling invisible. I was mired in an incredibly dense sense of darkness, the kind of darkness that's easy to disappear into if you are not careful. And I *wasn't* careful—I egged myself on. *Yes*, I told myself. *You do not matter.* If I didn't matter, I concluded, I quite obviously shouldn't exist.

In retrospect, the image of myself huddled over a laptop, searching YouTube for informative videos on "how to safely overdose," is morbidly funny to me, even though in the moment it was very much the opposite. It was during this search that I came across (or the Universe's algorithm arranged for me to see) a link to a Josephine Baker documentary on YouTube. I still don't know how, given the state of mind that I was in, I was able to muster the energy and the curiosity to click on the thumbnail, but I did.

I was astonished that America could produce such a person and then reject her. I was transported by the story of her life, her journey from poor St. Louis–born Freda Josephine McDonald to ~*Josephine Baker*~, the first international Black superstar. I was even more transported by the story of her body in movement, the signature dips and curls that catapulted her to fame in 1920s Paris. One clip in particular held me enough that I played it twice: an excerpt of Baker dancing in the 1927 film *La Revue des revues*. Just twenty-one, she is in the center of some chic cafe entirely populated with white patrons dressed in tuxedos and gowns.

Baker is dressed in something short and fringey with patches of what looks to be leopard skin. She is the most elegant, the chicest, the coolest woman in the room, her body moving with a rhythm and poetry that can only be described as Black. I remember watching her spiral and twirl and flip, contort her face into odd but satisfying expressions, her eyes suggesting a knowing sarcasm. I remember feeling lifted. The image of her spiraling body pulled me out of my own spiral. Knowing that someone like Baker had existed in the world I lived in lit something up inside me. When the documentary was over, I made a gesture toward existing, an assertion that I mattered, even if I didn't fully believe that yet. Social media has always been a great place for pretending, for playing, for projecting some idealized version of self. A way to hide in plain sight. I posted the selfie and the hashtag. An attempt to be carefree.

Turning to art and turning to Black women has always been the road by which I come back to myself. I collect images of Black women like precious jewels: Josephine Baker twirling; little Troy from *Crooklyn*, hair braided and beaded, smirking directly into the camera; Mel B of the Spice Girls with her pierced tongue stuck way out, kicking a leopard-print bell-bottom-clad leg high into the air; Marsha P. Johnson with red and yellow flowers in her hair, her smile resplendent; Audre Lorde standing in front of a chalkboard with the words "Women are powerful and dangerous" scrawled across it; the bones moving smoothly beneath the skin of my grandmother's hands as she pounded yam and cassava into *fufu*. These images, disparate and disconnected, are all expressions, in a sense, of who I am. That's what this book is about, too: how images of Black women have helped inform and form my own image of myself and allowed me to understand myself.

This book is also a meditation on a single idea: what it means to be a Black woman and truly be "carefree." What does it mean to define ourselves, to cling to our right to complexity, in spite of everything? Every essay in this book wrestles with that question—how can any one image, any one label, *any one hashtag*, properly convey this complexity?

The journey of Black women in the culture, of the culture, has been a fraught one. It has also been incredibly beautiful. Hopefully, whoever you are, reading this, you find inspiration in that beauty. And hopefully you are reminded that Black women are essential. Our stories are worth telling. Our stories are culturally and historically relevant, worthy of being shared, heard, awarded, nerded out over, explored, analyzed, debated, referenced, lovingly critiqued. Most of all, our stories are our own to tell.

As I write this, I'm thinking of the Black women whose influence has permeated throughout mainstream culture over the last several hundred years, the actors, writers, artists, curators, musicians, activists, athletes, and more who have healed me in some way, mostly just by existing. I'd like to name just some of these people, to hold a space of honor and gratitude for them. I encourage you to return to this page often and look up each name, one by one, whenever you need to feel inspired or seen or activated in some way: Althea Gibson, Dorothy Dandridge, Cicely Tyson, Claudette Colvin, Dr. Mae Jemison, Harriet Tubman, Ida B. Wells, Moms Mabley, Whitney Houston, Zora Neale Hurston, Octavia E. Butler, Bessie Smith, Florynce Kennedy, Lil' Kim, Thelma Golden, Melanie B, Queen Latifah, Madam C. J. Walker, Carrie Mae Weems, Julie Dash, Robin Givhan, Saidiya Hartman, Miss Major Griffin-Gracy, Trina McGee, Gabby Douglas, Nella Larsen, Cheryl Clarke, Shirley Chisholm, Yara Shahidi, Cree Summer, Tarana Burke,

Salt-N-Pepa, Kelis, Neneh Cherry, Octavia St. Laurent, Marsha P. Johnson, June Jordan, Lorraine Hansberry, Gladys Bentley, Tracey "Africa" Norman, Misty Copeland, Wilma Rudolph, Linda Martell, Yaba Blay, Mari Copeny, Thandiwe Newton, Nina Mae McKinney, Maya Angelou, Erykah Badu, Vilissa Thompson, Phyllis Hyman, Naomi Campbell, Pam Grier, Mary Church Terrell, Laverne Cox, Kasi Lemmons, Ethel Waters, Marielle Franco, Poly Styrene, Cheryl Dunye, Grace Jones, Toyin Ojih Odutola, Munroe Bergdorf, Genevieve Nnaji, Angela Bowen, Sojourner Truth, Gabourey Sidibe, Skin, Mariama Bâ, Shingai Shoniwa, Ruby Dee, Billie Holiday, Angela Davis, Ruth E. Carter, Eartha Kitt, Toni Morrison, Mahen Bonetti, Alice Coltrane, Serena Williams, SZA, Tracee Ellis Ross, Missy "Misdemeanor" Elliott, Aaron Philip, Josephine Baker, Ella Fitzgerald, Toni Cade Bambara, Patricia Okoumou, Aïssa Maïga, Tiffany Haddish, Phillis Wheatley, Assata Shakur, Nichelle Nichols, Angelica Ross, Faith Couch, Lupita Nyong'o, Junglepussy, Nikki Giovanni, Solange, Toyin Salau.

Finally, what this book is not: a history, an explainer, a guide, or a map to Blackness. There are some things I do not wish to overexplain because there is a freedom, an easiness, in not having to explain, and in inviting those who are unfamiliar to do the work on their own. There's a freedom, too, in not having all the answers. I'm straight, I'm cis, I don't have a visible disability. I came of age in America, but I am not African American. My experience is unique, thus my perspective is unique—but not definitive. This book does not aspire to define Black womanhood but to challenge and explore the tenuous definitions that already exist.

Most of all, most importantly, this book is an offering.

Althea Gibson

Althea Gibson: 1956; Library of Congress Prints
and Photographs Division, *New York World-Telegram*
and the *Sun* Newspaper Photograph Collection.

Bodies

I've been thinking about Lizzo's body. Not her physical body but the idea of her body as it exists in the minds of everyone but her. The body from which so much is extrapolated. Her body as an abstraction, a reflection of what folks really feel about themselves. I've been contemplating how exhausting and unfair the harmful meanings, narratives, responsibilities, and violences we place on bodies are. Especially bodies that are not our own.

Since her come up in 2016, Lizzo's body has been the running theme in the public conversations people have about her and her work as a music artist, if her work ever really comes up at all. On social media and gossip sites her fatness has been made into a blank screen onto which people project endless scrutiny and debate about respectability politics and double standards, body positivity and self-love.

In April 2020 Lizzo was a guest on Diddy's Instagram Live "dance-a-thon," an online event launched to raise money to aid those affected by COVID-19. Diddy had invited a cadre of famous friends, including Jennifer Lopez and Naomi Campbell, to virtually dance with him and his sons as millions of followers watched online. During her scheduled dance-off with the rapper-mogul, Lizzo, visibly elated to be participating, began to twerk. Diddy quickly shut her down.

"Whoa, whoa, whoa," he said, cutting off the music (Moneybagg Yo's "1 2 3"). "It's Easter Sunday. Let's play something a little more family friendly."

Lizzo seemed embarrassed, but, if she actually was, she quickly and gracefully regrouped. She suggested that they put on her hit song "Juice," and they continued dancing. That was that until, later in the day, Instagram/reality TV star Draya Michele joined Diddy's dance-a-thon and twerked to the song "Back That Azz Up" by Juvenile.

The visual of Draya, waist tinier and skin a little lighter than Lizzo's, twerking just hours after Lizzo had been told not to, instantly kindled an online debate. Some people called Diddy out for being fatphobic. How could he stop Lizzo from twerking while allowing the much smaller Draya to throw it back without incident? How had he not clocked that double standard? In response to the backlash, Diddy posted a video clarifying that he hadn't been trying to stop Lizzo from twerking, just the song of choice. The next night, during another Instagram Live hang with singer Tory Lanez on April 13, Lizzo herself defended Diddy from the criticism. "The music was explicit," she said. "[Diddy] didn't want songs about stuff I did saying [explicit words] being played around children."

If Lizzo felt OK about the interaction with Diddy, that's fair enough. At the time, when I saw the story begin to storm the blogs, I wasn't so much concerned about what Diddy's motivations were as I was with the reactions to the situation, to Lizzo herself. There were people calling Diddy out in Lizzo's defense, yes, but there were also as many people saying that she had been "doing too much" by twerking. Visible fat Black women in pop culture, should they exist at all, have always been deemed "too much," simply for being visible.

Lizzo's persona as a music artist has at various moments throughout her rise been described by the media as "body positive" or "fat positive." Some of her most popular singles, like "Truth Hurts" and "Juice," are ebullient odes to self-love and empowerment. Her stage performances often highlight the beauty of big bodies—not just her own, often in bedazzled leotards and colorful two-pieces, but her dancers' as well. Onstage, on magazine covers, on red carpets, Lizzo does not do the thing that fat Black women are often expected to do, which is to pretend that her body does not exist. There's a radicality to this to be sure. But outside of that, there isn't anything particularly different about Lizzo as a pop star as compared to any other pop star. Lizzo is conventionally attractive. She makes great, palatable, catchy pop music. Yet still, her fatness has become for some the most central part of her identity as an artist rather than just a key facet of her identity. Why?

She herself has questioned the preoccupation. In October 2020, on the Netflix interview series *My Next Guest Needs No Introduction with David Letterman*, she said of her rise to fame, "All people could talk about or think about was my size. I didn't like when people condemned me for it. And it also kind of rubbed me the wrong way when I was praised—'You're so brave!' . . . They thought they were complimenting me by saying that I was 'unapologetic.' What do I have to apologize for?" Fat Black women are always implicitly made to feel as though they have something to apologize for, and that something is daring to exist in a fat body.

So much of the narrative surrounding Lizzo is about her body and her bravery. The bravery of her body. The defiance. The *gall*. Never mind that there are women all over the country and indeed the planet who look just like Lizzo. Who are *bigger* than Lizzo. This narrative is a dangerous one, because it suggests that to be a fat woman is to be in a constant state of self-delusion, *tricking* yourself into loving yourself.

Of course, Lizzo isn't the first fat Black woman entertainer to push back against these ideas. There is a lineage of big Black women, especially in music, who have taken control of the visual narrative of their own bodies within the culture. Ma Rainey, Sister Rosetta Tharpe, Willa Mae "Big Momma" Thornton, Queen Latifah, Missy Elliott, and Brittany Howard of the Alabama Shakes are names that come to mind. But Lizzo's presence and her trajectory are largely emblematic of this particular moment in time, a simultaneous progression and regression in the way we view fat Black women's bodies in pop culture. In her music videos and on red carpets, she has the air of a woman perfectly at home in her body, in her sexuality, in her spirit. A woman who posts racy thirst traps and throws her ass onstage while soloing on the flute with wild and fervent abandon. A woman who doesn't give a fuck. At least, this is what has been ascribed to her.

Searching Lizzo's name on social media is a lesson in cruelty. Cruelty in the form of jokes and memes and general unsolicited comments about her size. Tweets like, "Not fat shaming but there's no way Lizzo smells good." "Lizzo is insanely fat and needs to put more clothes on forever." Memes like a picture of Lizzo performing onstage with big, bold white text over it that reads: "LIZZO'S SO FAT IT TOOK 15 MINUTES TO DOWNLOAD THIS IMAGE SO I COULD SHARE IT ON FACEBOOK."

And, in the comments section on her official Instagram page, among gushing praise from fangirls, are reactions like vomit emojis and statements like, for instance (in response to a video she posted in 2019 of herself and a friend twerking): "This is disgusting on another level" and "You're too big to be doing this."

That Lizzo is such a challenging pop culture figure, on the receiving end of so much hate, vitriol, and debate, speaks volumes about the ways we're taught to react to fat Black bodies. That Lizzo wearing a bikini while lounging on the beach, or twerking at a nightclub with her friends, or doing that outrageous pop-star shtick of showing up to a basketball game in a backless dress that reveals a bejeweled thong is considered not just outrageous but offensive or even truly subversive says that society's imagination when it comes to fat women is amazingly stagnant. From that stagnation grows harm.

In a TikTok video posted on December 12, 2020, Lizzo shared thoughts on the candid reality of her relationship with her body, a relationship more complex than some might have assumed. "I came home, I took a shower, and I just started having all of these really negative thoughts about myself like, what's wrong with me," she said. "Maybe all the mean things people say about me are true. Why am I so disgusting? Hating my body. And normally I would have some positive thing to say to get me out of this. But I don't and that's OK, too. I think these [thoughts] are normal, they happen to everybody . . . I know I'm beautiful. I just don't feel it."

A few days later, she posted another video of herself to social media, revealing the results of a ten-day smoothie detox, posing for the camera in black leggings and a cropped sports bra. There was an uproar. Several fat-positive bloggers lamented that Lizzo was not only buying into but promoting the toxicity of diet culture and fad diets.

One white woman blogger tweeted, "Lizzo is a fatphobe now." She added:

> My heart hurts with all my fat peers today. Even though she won't say it and will probably try to excuse it, I'm sorry that Lizzo did that to us. We are worthy and what she posted was so fucked. If you are triggered and upset by it I am right there with you.

The number of white women in particular who felt personally attacked by Lizzo's smoothie detox was fascinating. Black women's bodies are often made the vessel for everyone else's insecurities in ways that rob us of our agency, our complexity, and our humanity. That places a burden on us to make a way for others to find self-love. Why is Lizzo's complicated personal relationship to her own, highly visible, highly disrespected body seen as a betrayal? Why is it shocking to learn that she, a human being, a pop artist whose physical appearance is an integral part of her artistry, is as susceptible to the pressures and violences of fatphobia and diet culture as anyone else? Why simply critique her identity, motives, and ethics rather than critiquing the structures that implicitly made her feel the need to detox? You can point out the possible harm in what she did while also holding space for why she did it.

At some point, Lizzo was distilled down to a Sassy Fat Black Woman with no feelings, whose body exists only to either shock or inspire you. When people heard her words of encouragement on the stage at the 2019 MTV Video Music Awards, where, flanked by beautiful fat Black dancers, she said, "It's so hard trying to love yourself in a world that doesn't love you back. So I want to take this opportunity right now to just feel *good as hell*, we deserve to feel good as hell," no one considered that the message wasn't just for the audience but also for herself.

Meaning is often placed on Black women's bodies without our consent or cooperation. There is a kind of violence to this, and this is how representation politics always falter. Lizzo declares that she loves herself and her body and she's criticized for "promoting" an unhealthy lifestyle. Lizzo declares that she struggles to love herself and her body, to find healthy ways of relating and caring for that body, and she's criticized for promoting diet culture. In all of this, her actual message, which is that she is a human being, is completely ignored.

What sense does it make to be angry at Lizzo for supposedly failing to be the perfectly infallible patron saint of fat positivity that she never explicitly claimed to be? Pop culture rarely makes room for empathy, much less so when Black women are concerned. Where is the empathy?

In January 2020, when fitness guru Jillian Michaels

came under fire for asking "why are we celebrating [Lizzo's] body?" during a BuzzFeed interview, she unknowingly exhibited the insidious subtlety of this harm.

"Why does [Lizzo's body] matter?" Michaels (the adoptive mother of a young Black girl) asked.

Really, implicitly, she was asking, "*How* can Lizzo's body matter? If Lizzo's body matters, does that mean there's a world that exists in which self-love isn't conditional? A world in which people don't have to be in constant judgment of themselves and others in order to be happy, successful, whole? And if that's true, does that mean every bad thing I've been made to feel and think about fat people (and fat people have been made to feel and think about themselves) is a lie?"

The answer, obviously: a resounding yes.

Hating your body is a spiritual disaster that begins with witnessing the ways bodies that look like yours are ignored, abused, condemned.

When *Moesha*, the '90s sitcom that starred Brandy at the height of her teen queen fame, began streaming on Netflix, I rushed to rewatch the series and revel in sweet, uncomplicated nostalgia. All I could focus on, however, were the pervasive fat jokes aimed throughout the show at Countess Vaughn, who played Moesha's best friend, Kim Parker.

Minutes into season one, episode one, Kim asks, "Do you think I need to lose weight, Mo?"

Moesha hesitates, laughs, and answers, "Girl, you got a cute face!!"

These kinds of quips riddled the series, particularly in the early seasons. Kim—a fifteen-year-old girl when we first meet her in season one—was constantly on the receiving end of jokes and gags about her size, usually from her own friends and sometimes even from adults. Her function, as sidekick, was to cheerfully take on abuse from her friends, and thus the audience. In episode two of the first season, Moesha and Kim experience a rift when Kim learns Moesha is talking about her (and her size) behind her back. They eventually make up, of course. But the fat jokes, both subtle and overt, continue throughout the series.

Kim Parker is part of a long tradition of so-called sassy fat Black women in film and TV (particularly from the 1990s, 2000s, and 2010s) who functioned largely to provide funny one-liners and be the butt of jokes, usually about their size or intelligence. Their fatness was used as an excuse to turn them into visual and hypothetical punchlines. Beloved comedians and filmmakers have made entire careers off of parodying fat Black women. Gabourey Sidibe was lauded and received an Academy Award nomination for her stellar work in *Precious*, and yet the name of her character, Precious, has become derogatory, an insult. *"Plus yo, my bitch make your bitch look like Precious,"* Kanye West says in the third verse of the song "Mercy."

Fat Black women have been desexualized and

relegated to the roles of sassy one-liner generators or wise advice givers, a tradition dating all the way back to Black "mammy" characters of old. Or, if they are at all sexual, this is usually played for laughs (HBO's *Insecure*, radical in so many ways in terms of its depictions of sexual Black women, has fallen into this trap with the character of Kelli in early seasons). And, if their sexuality isn't necessarily played for laughs, it is fetishized, or it's held up as a kind of anomaly, an impossibility, a novel thing, something to gawk at rather than celebrate. The rare instances when this is not the case seem to slip the collective consciousness.

I remember back in 2018, Mo'Nique, the comedian/ actress who came to mainstream prominence playing Countess Vaughn's mother on *The Parkers*, had to gather actress Rebel Wilson after the latter had claimed she was the "first-ever plus-sized girl to be the star of a romantic comedy." Wilson said this on *The Ellen Show* in promotion of the film *Isn't It Romantic*, which was in fact not the first film to hold this distinction.

Several Black women pointed this out on social media. What about Queen Latifah in *Last Holiday* or Mo'Nique in *Phat Girlz*, movies that had both been released in 2006? Wilson's first inclination was to double down on her comments on Twitter, suggesting that the classification of these movies existed in "a grey area" and that it was questionable as to whether "technically those actresses were plus size when filming those movies." She then went on a blocking spree, ignoring several Black women who critiqued her initial comment and challenged her excuses, preventing them from engaging with her.

That is, until Mo'Nique replied: "Let's please not allow this business to erase our talent with giving grey areas and technicalities. Take a moment and know the history. DON'T BE A PART OF ERASING IT. I wish you the best."

The whole affair ended as these things always do, with a carefully crafted PR apology via Twitter on November 5 in which Wilson stated, "In a couple of well-intentioned moments, hoping to lift my fellow plus sized women up, I neglected to show the proper respect to those who climbed this mountain before me like Mo'Nique, Queen Latifah, Melissa McCarthy, Ricki Lake and likely many others."

I could guess why these films might have slipped Wilson's mind—films that center Black women of any kind as romantic leads are designated "Black films" and thus not to be actually included in the canon of romantic comedies.

(Wilson would later go on to reveal significant weight loss, which was met with mostly positivity and headlines like "Rebel Wilson Reflects on Her 'Uphill Journey' Following 60-Pound Weight Loss in 2020" and "Rebel Wilson Says These 7 Things Helped Her Get Healthy." The most wearying thing about double standards is how predictable they are.)

There's a cultural misconception that fat Black women are more comfortable with their fatness, less susceptible to the pain of fatphobia, generally more accepted. This misconception springs from the very erasure Rebel Wilson put on display with her comments. It's true that fat white women experience their own kind of erasure in pop culture—in movies and TV shows they are rarely the main love interest, always the sad fat girl pining for the leading man's affections à la Janeane Garofalo in *The Truth About Cats and Dogs*. If she wins those affections, it's because she's somehow transformed herself to meet a specific ideal, or because the male protagonist, out of the goodness of his heart, has decided to overlook her so-called flaws. But the fat Black woman is desexualized altogether. There isn't even the hope, the implication, of romance or sexual pleasure or adoration for her. Her sexuality is the joke.

These characters rarely have storylines or arcs that don't revolve around the main character, and if they do, these arcs are inconsequential to the piece as a whole. And yet, without these characters, nothing else works. This was the case with Countess Vaughn as Kim. Vaughn, a veteran of sitcom television who had starred on the show *227* in 1988, had an innate ability to steal scenes on *Moesha* while simultaneously elevating everyone else on screen. In less capable hands, Kim would have come off as cloying and parodic, the Black girl Screech of the crew. Instead, Vaughn imbued her with a warmth and a realness that made her not only funny but incredibly endearing—far more endearing, in fact, than the titular character herself.

Vaughn was apparently aware of how integral she was to the show, and this infamously created tension on set. In a 1998 profile in *VIBE* magazine, Brandy said of Vaughn:

> I think she's very funny, very talented. I just feel like she wants to be in the position I'm in. People tell her, "You're the reason why the show's successful." And she's told me that before. And she's called me a bitch—to my face. She said, "I'm the reason why the show is successful, bitch." In front of a lot of people. And I looked at her like, "Wow." I couldn't say nothing about her because I wasn't about to . . . She knows. She wakes up and looks at herself in the mirror and gets disgusted. I don't.

The tension between Brandy and Vaughn, as evidenced in Brandy's quote, got so bad that a compromise was made: Vaughn would leave *Moesha* for her own spinoff, *The Parkers*. With Mo'Nique co-starring, the show became an equally big hit, running for five seasons and drawing 3.6 million viewers for its finale episode in 2004.

And so it seems, in spite of it all, Vaughn kind of won. She was able to parlay a beloved if disrespected character into her own successful show. But then what? After *The Parkers* ended, Vaughn's career largely stalled. This is typical of many TV stars, of course, but especially for stars such as Vaughn: Black women who, though talented, don't fit the arbitrary Hollywood standards of whiteness and thinness.

After just a handful of guest spots throughout the 2000s, Vaughn came back into the Black Twitter zeitgeist in 2014 as a cast member of the TV One reality show *Hollywood Divas*. On the show, which also starred *Girlfriends* actor Golden Brooks, Vaughn revealed that she became pregnant at eighteen, just as *The Parkers* was beginning.

"I had an unwanted pregnancy. I had just started my TV show," she said. "I knew that in Black Hollywood a girl having a baby, they'd get rid of you."

She added, "I had to make a decision to get rid of the child for my career because I knew from the jump that if I let any of them know what was going on, they would have canceled my show."

Vaughn made a decision that many other young women have had to make, getting an abortion for the sake of her career and her future. Her experience, though, also underscored the precariousness of being an actor like her at the time that she got the spinoff. There was a sense that she couldn't miss this chance because she'd probably never get another one like it again. Perhaps this was true.

It's always tempting and easy to do the thing we all do when we look back at the objects of our nostalgia, that thing where you pick apart all the ways in which something from the past was problematic. This kind of looking back can be useful, as long as it doesn't turn into some sort of exercise in making ourselves feel morally superior to a past that we were a part of. Instead, we should look back as a way to understand the ramifications of harmful tropes and the ways we've integrated these stereotypes into real life. I wonder how those fat jokes showed up in the world. And how did Vaughn feel about them?

So many people have, in retrospect, recognized how amazing Vaughn's singing was on the show, how she should have released an album. Which makes me think about the time she made a serious foray into music in 2016 with the release of a single called "Do You Love Him?" The song's video quickly became fodder for hilarious memes and parodies. I definitely laughed along. But I see, now, that much of the laughter at her expense was tangled up with a common tendency to not take big Black women seriously, a tendency that impedes careers, diminishes opportunities. How many more Countess Vaughns are we not talking about?

I'm contemplating an entire generation of Black girls, myself among them, watching *Moesha* and swallowing that stealthy hatred whole, not realizing the poison we were ingesting. How does that manifest itself in a life? What kind of little self-betrayals does it inspire? What harmful ways of seeing myself and my body have I unknowingly latched onto since I was a girl?

And what alternate reality could I be living in had I been aware of more depictions of fat Black girls and women being loved, desired, cherished, valued beyond their capacity to be a good sidekick or a punching bag for our collective insecurities? Would that have saved me from the gnawing fear that my value and ultimately my safety are contingent on 20 lbs of fat? Would that have soothed my desire to be smaller, to literally take up less space in the world? Would that have changed anything at all?

I'm thinking about Black women's bodies and the disrespect that seems to come with existing in one. The disrespect that seeps into our souls and makes us accomplices to our own demise. The disrespect that implicitly encourages us to hate ourselves, that coaxes us into settling for less than we deserve in every facet of our lives. The disrespect that ultimately breeds the kind of self-neglect that you don't even realize is self-neglect until it's too late. I'm thinking about how to fight that.

Around 2018 I got fat. Depressed and binge eating to the point of physical pain, I rapidly went from 165 lbs to 200 lbs, then 220, then 240. All this in a year. I hadn't even realized I was gaining weight until it was all there, and the only clothes that would fit my form were leggings, big t-shirts, and long, shapeless dresses. Quite suddenly, I had to reckon with everything that I had ever internalized and externalized about my body. I had always thought of myself as "fat," in the dysmorphic way that so many femmes whose bodies do not strictly conform to the thin ideal think of themselves as "fat." But now I was a different kind of fat, the kind of fat that other people could perceive, the kind of fat that was objectively recognizable.

I've always regarded my body as a benevolent stranger, so confronting this new version of my body intimately was the absolute last thing I wanted to do. Gaining that amount of weight in such a short period of time was traumatic and disorienting in ways I simply hadn't been prepared for. And so I dealt with my new body by pretending that it did not exist. I like to dress up. Before the weight gain, I would post weekly outfit pics on my Instagram. This came to an abrupt stop. It wasn't even so much what people would think of me as it was what I would think of myself, acknowledging this new change, broadcasting myself clumsily trying to figure out how to dress this new body.

You find other ways to avoid the body: by never leaving the house, by disappearing into sleep in the middle of the day so as to feel weightless. I'd go through cycles of binge-eating, a ritual that was equal parts self-punishment and self-soothing, a way to numb myself with the good, uncomplicated feeling that food gave me. I would spend hours on end lying very still in my bed or on my sofa, disappearing into movies and YouTube videos long enough to forget myself entirely. I'd scroll through Instagram and come across photos of beautiful fat Black women like Stephanie Yeboah, like Kellie Brown, like Lizzo—and wonder, fleetingly, why I could see beauty in their bodies but not my own.

Then I'd hit "like" and keep scrolling.

Internalized fatphobia is all about a rejection of the self, scrolling past our insecurities instead of facing them head on. I've analyzed and scrutinized and picked myself apart so much over the course of my life that now when I see an image of myself—a picture, a video, my reflection in a mirror—I do not see me. Instead I see a soft pile of neuroses and insecurities, and I can't tell which parts of this pile are actually me and which parts are products of the negative things I've been implicitly encouraged by the world to believe about myself.

I remember shopping for new clothes the winter after I gained weight (for a function that I had desperately tried to but couldn't get out of), standing before a large dressing room mirror, stripping off my clothes slowly and hesitantly, and staring at what my body was, for what it was. I remember I felt afraid. I couldn't understand *why* I felt afraid, what exactly I was afraid of, but I knew it was not simply the sight of my body, the stripes and dimples and rolls in new places, the latticework of fresh stretch marks on my ass. Perhaps it was a fear of not really being able to see myself, the fear that I never really would.

In *Fearing the Black Body: The Racial Origins of Fat Phobia,* Dr. Sabrina Strings writes: "The fear of the imagined 'fat black woman' was created by racial and religious ideologies that have been used to both degrade black women *and* discipline white women." It's this imagined fat Black woman I was looking at, this figure and form created to terrorize, control, and restrain all of us, to teach us that fatness is synonymous with laziness is synonymous with sickness is synonymous with Blackness.

Fear is a key ingredient in the formation of race. Fear and shame go hand in hand. The modern-day obsession with being skinny, or being "acceptably" fat (pear shaped, with a smaller waist, a thick ass, and rolls tucked away), links all the way back to the very roots of slavery, of anti-Blackness. The shaming of fat Black women, of fat people in general, has never been about our beauty or even our health. It has always been about power.

That power, I'm finding, delegates so much about how we live our lives, the things we feel we're allowed to indulge in. I've been so scared of existing in my body, in documenting my body as it is now, that I've denied myself things that make me feel good about myself and felt guilty in instances where I've actually allowed myself to feel pleasure. It happens when I eat a delicious meal and go back for seconds. It happens when I have sex. It happens when I rest. A rush of something like shame washes over me, and I quietly admonish myself for overindulging. Why? Fat Black bodies in states of pleasure, that aren't used as punchlines or for shock value, are few and far between in the larger culture. So this signals that fat Black bodies are not deserving of pleasure or joy of any kind. So then I feel like my body isn't deserving of pleasure, except, maybe, for the pleasure of eating, but even that becomes fraught.

Black women are in a precarious placement, attacked

from all sides. One could produce charts and studies and percentages about the unique discrimination fat Black women experience in the job market, the medical racism that is systemically killing fat Black women at alarming rates. We battle for self-esteem and self-worth in a world that believes many of us are imbued with some sort of innate, supernatural self-esteem that magically shields us from the bullshit. Never mind that the acceptance of fat Black women is usually contingent on what emotional or physical labor can be performed: to nurture, to make you laugh, to inspire you.

Everything that I've internalized about fat bodies has made me less inclined to show my body care. Sometimes I look at old pictures of myself and cannot believe how much pain that body held, and continues to hold, and how much that pain distorted what I see when I look in the mirror. The body positivity movement has been difficult for me to fully embrace. I think the emphasis on the body is at least part of my problem. But it feels far more radical to attempt to see myself as beautiful, my body as worthy, rather than to feel neutral about it. To feel neutral about my body is to say that it does not matter, and part of my survival means embracing/emphasizing that it does.

White supremacy terrorizes oppressed people by forcing them to be complicit in their own oppression. This is because white supremacy, from which I believe all of the fuckery of this life ultimately springs, lacks imagination. The goal of white supremacy is to kill your sense of imagination, too. White supremacy cannot make sense of Black bodies, fat bodies, disabled bodies, dark-skinned bodies, trans bodies, gender non-conforming bodies—indeed any body that does not conform—without placing them within a hierarchy of value. White supremacy is the opposite of empathy. White supremacy says empathy, care, tenderness, joy, pleasure, opportunity, *freedom,* should only be available to a finite group of people. White supremacy says that empathy should be totally incumbent on the way you look, and the way you look, always, should be beautiful.

Empathy should not be incumbent on beauty or desirability. Desirability should not be the only criterion for being valued. Your desirability should not be a matter of life and death. Beauty and desirability are subjective and, in many cases, totally irrelevant. Certainly in the case of empathy. In any case, so-called undesirable people deserve empathy, love, and care.

This notion of desirability, of who gets to be given a fuck about, is inextricably linked with white supremacy. And it always boils down to white supremacy, doesn't it? White supremacy focuses keenly on the body as a metric for worth. White supremacy is mired in the trap of the body. Even body positivity, put forth as a good thing but now co-opted by the mainstream and increasingly depoliticized, falls into this trap, placing more importance on how we feel about our bodies as opposed to how we feel about our souls.

My relationship to my own body, as I've mentioned

before, has always been incredibly fraught. Gaining a significant amount of weight only heightened that. That tense relationship is tangled up with the terror of being a Black woman, of feeling as though my body is not only disposable to society at large, but also in some sense not my own. In this umpteenth reckoning America seems to be having with the reality of Black death, I've realized that so much of the anxiety I feel around being seen is not arbitrary. All my life, I've wanted proximity to beauty because I implicitly understood that, as a dark-skinned Black woman, my survival depended on how I look in every sense of the word.

This is what I've been doing all my life, I now realize: striving for perfection as a means to access safety, care, empathy. But a life spent striving for perfection as a means to access safety is not a life at all. If my teens and twenties were about conforming and contorting, my thirties have been about figuring out a technology of self-making that has nothing to do with desirability or, if it does, a personal desirability, an exploration of how I desire myself.

I believe that our personal relationship with our bodies has implications on society as a whole. Fatphobia guides us all in not having empathy for bodies that do not conform, but it also guides us in not having empathy for ourselves. Me gaining weight was never the problem, the problem was the punishment I wrought on my body for failing to conform and the lack of empathy I had for myself in this struggle.

And so I'm trying to push against that. I'm trying to imagine a new world for myself and thus a new world entirely. One in which I can honor my body while acknowledging the specter of violence—both physical and psychological violence—that seems to haunt it constantly. Realizing that the body is constantly deteriorating, changing, stretching, shrinking, sagging, wrinkling—the self-hatred that makes looking in a mirror while I'm naked is its own kind of body horror. But what about re-creating myself, refashioning my body without necessarily changing the way it looks? But by rejecting all that is projected upon it? Is that even possible?

I'm imagining a world where I can leave my apartment in torn flip-flops and a stained muumuu with my hair looking wild and unkempt and not feel self-conscious about (a) feeling ugly, "unpresentable," and (b) fearing that because I don't look "put together" I'll be more susceptible to harm. And I'm imagining, perhaps most fervently, a world where I can have empathy for myself even when no one else does.

Some time ago I filmed some content for a popular beauty brand. I had recently cut off all my hair, and there was nowhere for my double chin to hide. Someone saw me in the ad on Instagram, excitedly tagged me. I went to look at the video and cringed. Then I saw the comments—mostly very sweet and positive, but of course my mind and heart zeroed in on the few comments where people were making fun of my appearance, leaning on fatphobic and transphobic language to do so. One person called me "Precious," and another commented, simply, "This is a man."

When I was younger, something like this would have resulted in me shutting down for the rest of the day. But, that day, it stung but not for so long. This is hard to always remember, but it is true: being genuinely kind to yourself means learning to not internalize how people who don't know you and/or don't care for you feel about you. A concept.

It is amazing to exist in a Black body, to exist in a body at all. There is an undeniable beauty in it. To be alive in this body when so many other Black women are not, to remember that and hold on to that, is humbling. But it can also be terrifying, because to exist in a Black body is to exist in a persistent state of precarity, to be in constant anticipation of some form of violence. And so, at least for me, so much of the process of learning to love this body has been in learning to find *safety* in this body, no matter its form. I want the way I exist in this body (the way you, reader, exist in your body), to be more than an act of defiance.

I want my existence to be affirming, celebratory, complicated, beautiful, real. As a Black woman, my relationship to my body has larger implications. Shifting the way I feel about my fatness compels me to confront the way I feel about other Black women's bodies and think critically about the things I project onto bodies that are not my own, bodies that do and do not look like mine. I'm trying. Stepping fully into a place where you want to demand the right to exist from the only authority on the matter that matters, yourself, is a process that progresses by degrees, that's complicated by the machine constantly working to grind us down. It doesn't happen all at once, but gradually. It is an accumulation of little wins mixed with little losses. It's a process that we see Lizzo navigating publicly, but a process so many of us privately share.

I am still working through it. I give myself permission to struggle. I grant myself the grace to. I'm allowing myself to mourn the body I thought I needed to feel whole, to feel seen. That body never existed, and if it ever did, its existence was always meant to be fleeting. Something that has become clear to me in the process of processing is that bodies are transient, miraculous, ephemeral, and *precious*. The beauty in bodies is that they change. This seems basic, but it's a concept so difficult to hold on to sometimes. I may lose weight or gain weight, have a baby, cut my hair, whatever, but what that means for me is what it means for *me*.

And so, a mantra:

I reject the harmful meanings, narratives, responsibilities, and violences that have been placed on my body, by myself and others. I reject whatever harmful narratives I've knowingly and unknowingly placed on the bodies of others. I reject every image of a fat Black woman I have ever seen that has suggested, either implicitly or explicitly, that she is undeserving of visibility, rest, pleasure, joy, care, empathy. I embrace the fact that the struggle is real, and always will be. I embrace, always, the knowledge that my body is my own.

Theatrical poster for the film
Carmen Jones (1954)

Dorothy Dandridge: Theatrical poster for the film *Carmen Jones*, 1954.

She's a Freak

*Society has a big issue with women who find ways
to monetize men's desires. Yet male dominated industries
have been attaching a price tag to women's bodies
and sex appeal for centuries.*
—MUNROE BERGDORF

I created my first online dating profile when I was around twenty-one, on OkCupid. The profile was made from a place of quiet desperation. I was a virgin who had never had a boyfriend or even been kissed. I was over it. I regarded myself as a perennially awkward woman-child, too afraid to flirt with, let alone talk to, anyone that I was attracted to in the real world. What stopped me from putting myself out there was a mixture of things. Low self-esteem, debilitating shyness, and a near-pathological fear of a very specific form of rejection: rejection for being a dark-skinned, not-skinny, 4C-natural-haired Black girl in a heterosexual dating scene that to my mind seemed to privilege anyone who was anything but.

But I came of age on the internet, an adolescent and twenty-something of the LiveJournal and Tumblr eras, back when social media still felt like a safe haven for me, a place where I could play and also where I could enact some control. And so an internet dating profile, I thought, was the optimal way to explore the potential of dating (and ultimately the potential of pleasure) on my own introverted terms. From my laptop, I uploaded a series of pictures that I hoped would subtly tell a story of me as a specific kind of person: an image of my twenty-one-year-old self, smiling coyly at the camera, wearing an intentionally hole-y David Bowie tee. Another image of me standing triumphantly over a large Thanksgiving spread that I hadn't cooked. For my About Me, I wrote a carefully curated list of my favorite movies that was deliberately equal parts highbrow and ironic. "I love Paul Thomas Anderson, Spike Lee, and *Titanic*."

I was satisfied with what I had come up with in thirty minutes. I saved the profile. I waited. Five minutes or so passed before I received my first message, which felt surprisingly fast, and promising. Based on the pictures on his profile, the message was from a thirty-something-year-old white dude who owned several pairs of cargo shorts. If I had a type, he was in no way it. But I opened the message anyway, thinking, "Well. Maybe?"

"Is it true what they say?" The message read. "Are you a freak? I bet you can twerk, too, huh?"

I tried to discern whether or not he was being serious and which would actually be worse: intentional or oblivious ignorance. I stared into the blue-white glow of my phone, dejected but mostly just annoyed by the banal offensiveness of the message. It was something that I had experienced in so many ways before, this condition of being whittled down, seen not as a person but the approximation of a person, a collection of body parts that just happen to make up a human being.

The OkCupid message struck me as a kind of echo of something that happened when I was around thirteen, walking home from school at the height of summer on a day nearing 100 degrees Fahrenheit. That day, I was wearing a baggy, long-sleeved top and black tights under a short skirt because I would have rather risked dying from heat stroke than have anyone see my arms, thighs, and legs in broad daylight. Changing in ways I couldn't understand or even really begin to articulate, my body was a site of profound shame. I found myself constantly wrestling with having a body, constantly wrestling with both fear and fascination, disgust and attraction. The only way, up until then, that I had figured out to cope with this was by pretending my body didn't exist, that pain didn't exist, that pleasure didn't exist, not really. Denying myself comfort in my body—by doing things like wearing too much fabric in sweltering hot weather—was a way to enact this philosophy of survival in my everyday life.

As I rounded a corner onto my street, a group of guys hanging out on the stoop of a house a few doors down from mine, in other words my neighbors, called out, laughing, "Bitch, ain't you hot?"

Another guy said, "She's probably a freak, she's probably thick as hell under all that." I receded further inside myself, embarrassed by how embarrassed I was of my own body, embarrassed because a part of me, in that moment, felt like shit, because I wasn't "thick" and that, too, made me feel bad about myself. In that moment, in these moments, I've often felt less like a person and more like the idea of a person. The idea of a thigh, an ass, a pair of breasts. The projections and expectations and assumptions placed on my body—*she's probably a freak*—make me feel out of control.

This lack of control, this quality of feeling your body and your being reduced from person to thing, is a rite of passage for so many femme-presenting people. There's an inevitability to this in a world that deems the body as the locus of the self. For Black women, our personhood—our bodies, our sexuality, and how others interpret and define the sexual potentiality of our bodies—has always been fraught. It's a history we carry with us even when we don't realize that we do, a history we inherit, a kind of memory that we may not be able to access but that many of us, regardless of background and history, can still feel, deeply, inside.

This history of dehumanization, particularly in the United States, has often been defined by certain caricatures of Black women and their bodies, for example, "the Jezebel." The first Jezebel was not a Black woman but a biblical Phoenician princess, first mentioned in the Old Testament's Book of Kings. This Jezebel, who single-handedly destroyed the lives of powerful men, became emblematic of feminine evil—a cunning temptress bringing men to ruin by way of her sexuality, her body a literal weapon. "Jezebel" has been applied to varying groups of women, but it has taken on especially loaded, especially lethal connotations when applied to Black women.

The Jezebel in this specific racial context is many things. For one, she is easy. She wants it too much. It is in her nature to want it. It is in her nature to want it just as it is in her nature to give it away. This is the primary function and state of the Black woman as a sexual being under a white supremacist lens. She is built to seduce. She is a "freak." The proportions of her body, ample breasts, abundant ass, are interpreted as objects designed to entice even as they repel.

The Black woman as Jezebel has deep roots in the rotted soil all racist ideologies in America take root in—chattel slavery. From the moment white Europeans crossed an ocean and stepped foot on African soil, Black bodies were regarded not only as commodities but as exotic objects to be lasciviously prodded and gawked at. This was a tactic, a means with which to perpetuate the idea that a Black body was an object to be coveted and possessed and that was simply the natural order of things.

So when we talk about the sexuality of Black women

throughout the diaspora, especially Black women in the Americas who descended from enslaved peoples, we must always remember this: Black women's bodies were once legally considered property. They were bought and sold, traded, loaned. Their bodies were put on display. They were placed on auction blocks, naked and oiled, to be appraised and examined by white buyers. Often this examination included the violating exploration of their breasts and their genitals. There was a vile eroticism to this, the calculating duality of the white gaze that could, from moment to moment and then all at once, project desire or distaste onto Black bodies.

It was merely a prelude, of course, to the further violation that would happen later. A white slave master having sex with his Black slaves without their consent was, in the eyes of the law, not rape. The law asked, disingenuously: How can a piece of property be raped? Black women were therefore assumed to be always sexually available, and this way of seeing them was sanctioned by the American government in its legal safeguarding of the institution of slavery and the rights of the slave owner. Often, it was even encouraged by the culture. Sexual virility was a sign of peak masculinity—there are reported cases of white slave-owning fathers encouraging, orchestrating, and even joining in the rape of enslaved women with their sons. Another kind of rite of passage. The sexual abuse of enslaved persons, both men and women, was rampant, and Black women's de facto sexual availability was set up in stark contrast to white women, who were propped up as paragons of purity and propriety.

In these ways, slavery perpetuated sexual misconceptions of Black women and men, reducing them to unpaid laborers and breeders whose bodies were valuable merely for labor, generating more slaves, suckling and caring for white children, and supplying forced sexual gratification for white people.

During the Jazz Age, the Black woman's body was molded and packaged into many forms. Caricatured, kitschy, and racist figurines of Black women were in vogue during the early part of the twentieth century—everything from ashtrays to wine glasses to butter dishes. These mundane items would be made into grotesque parodies: Black women were depicted not only with the tar-black skin, bugged eyes, and big lips consistent with racist Black iconography of the day but also often in the nude with exaggerated proportions, including huge buttocks and large, sagging breasts. The aim was clear: to depict Black women as not only sexually available but also sexually abhorrent—unattractive, almost grotesquely exotic. (Today, these items are still coveted and sought after by avid collectors.)

There are reverberations of the Jezebel throughout pop culture. She has many names and forms. Colloquially and culturally she has transformed but remains with us as the freak, the skeezer, the chickenhead, the ho, the bitch. She is Lydia Brown, a "mulatto" housekeeper in *Birth of a Nation* (played in Blackface by a white actress) who is uncontrollably sexually aroused by the stern orders from the white man she serves in every sense of the word. She is the nameless Black cis and trans women sex workers with two lines (at most) peppered throughout the Blaxploitation films of the 1970s and gritty, critically lauded crime dramas like *Taxi Driver*, and countless episodes of *Law & Order* in its many iterations. She is the anonymous vixen in the rap videos of the '80s, '90s, and 2000s. She is the porn performer featured in Pornhub videos with titles like "Black Bitch Gets Fucked" or "Ghetto Black Slut Sucks White Dick" or in movies like the rare and disturbing 1985 porno *Let Me Tell You About Black Chicks*, which features the simulation of three Black women being raped by Ku Klux Klan members.

There is another side to this coin, too, a kind of desexualization of Black women that in American culture specifically finds its roots in the archetype of the sexless mammy, undesired and undesiring. She is Hattie McDaniel in *Gone with the Wind*, and she is also every Black best friend in every teen comedy from the '90s and 2000s who never gets to be the love interest. She is the sassy fat Black woman sidekick whose sexual interiority is either invisible or implicitly played for laughs. Think of Retta as Donna on *Parks and Rec*, where she served up zingy one-liners about all the great sex she has and all the hot dudes she dates who remain nameless and faceless throughout the series, rendering her sexuality as an abstract punchline and nothing more. Think of Da'Vine Joy Randolph as Cherise in the TV adaptation of *High*

Fidelity, a character on a show about love and sex who was left completely out of that conversation despite ample opportunity to explore or at the very least *acknowledge* her sexuality in a tangible way.

I outline all of the above, even though it's painful, even though it may feel like a lot, even though if you are a Black woman reading this you're already keenly aware of it (and if you aren't, you honestly should be), because it is important that we remember that it is this history, this context, this lens through which Black women's bodies and their sexuality has been regarded. This is the fate, it seems, of a Black woman: to either be mammyfied, and have her sexuality completely stripped from her, or to be overtly sexualized without her consent. In all cases, her agency and her autonomy are taken from her. Is it any wonder, then, that this historic trauma has permeated the bodies of Black women and impacted how those bodies exist in the world?

I understand, and am deeply grateful for, the fact that in spite of this history Black women have still strived to assert agency and autonomy over their bodies, to explore sexuality through their own lenses and no one else's. Because in light of all these interpretations and depictions of Black women's bodies, the obvious question of how Black women have reclaimed their bodies arises. Art and pop culture have often served as rich ground for reclamation.

Black women have been expressing and asserting their sexuality through art for centuries—in spite of the histories that attempted to bind them into rigid roles. Here I'm thinking of erotic-fiction writer Zane and her books that center Black female pleasure. Or the tenderness with which seventeen-year-old Alike's sexual awakening as a queer woman is handled in Dee Rees' film *Pariah* (2011). Or the sex scenes on HBO's *Insecure*, where Black bodies and Black pleasure are centered, handled with care, and shown in all their flaws and perfections, specifically through the eyes of its main character, Issa.

Or that one particular image by artist Carrie Mae Weems in 1988, "Portrait of a Woman Who Has Fallen From Grace." Weems sits at the head of a bed, a burning cigarette dangling from her fingers. Her legs are wide open, partially covered by a white dress. She looks straight at you.

I'm also thinking of the word "thot," a word that has already begun to sag with age, but a word that comes so readily to my mind when I consider the concept of reclamation, when I think about looking *straight back* at the unsolicited interpretation and meaning placed on my own body. Images do one thing, after all. Words do another.

One week in 2018, the terms "niggerfishing" and "blackfishing" became a hot topic on social media. The phrases were coined and popularized by Black feminist writer Wanna Thompson and Twitter user @yeahboutella (also known as Deja, account since suspended) and referred to the concept of white women influencers purposely presenting themselves as Black or mixed with the use of heavy foundation several shades too dark and traditional Black hairstyles, a kind of Blackface for the social media age. Through the deception of bronzer and tanning lotion, these women amassed large Instagram and Twitter followings, and the lucrative money and sponsorships that go with that kind of online popularity—the Kardashians have made an art out of this particular scam.

Being one of the few Black opinion writers in my mostly white newsroom at the time, it unsurprisingly fell to me to whip up a reaction to the rapidly moving conversation, a piece that ended up with the tongue-in-cheek headline, "I Can't Stop Laughing at These Blackface Thots." The headline did not go over well with everyone. I received criticism from some people for using "Blackface thots" in the headline instead of using Thompson and Deja's term "Blackfishing," a critique that I understood.

But I was struck by another criticism I received, specifically of the word "thot." I was called out for using a misogynistic term, tantamount to calling these women— Blackface or no Blackface—sluts. I had to sit with that criticism and, in doing so, contemplate what I meant by using the word "thot," what thot really means, and for whom.

"Thot" was born out of AAVE and emerged in the zeitgeist and on the internet via hip-hop songs somewhere circa 2014, and it has been commonly agreed to be a shortened version of the phrase "that ho over there." Under this iteration of the word, a "thot" is a woman who is sexually available to men.

I can't deny that—outside of the specific context I was talking about in the article—"thot" is a word that has overwhelmingly been used to describe Black women, and not always in an empowered sense. And yet, I'm fascinated by the term, and the Black women who decide to claim it, especially the young "thots" of Instagram who, good or bad, have leveraged their looks for likes and followers, and their likes and followers for money and clout. There is a power in language, a power in the ways in which words like thot rise and fall and become integrated into the culture, and then co-opted.

At this point, thot has uniquely transcended its initially derogatory meaning, just as so many slurs used toward women have the potential to do (slut, heaux, etc.). When Cardi B declares, for instance, "I'm that East Coast Lit Thot!" on her track "Lit Thot," I know she's saying it with a sense of pride. I see the image that the word, in her use, conjures: one of a woman who has fallen from grace and is twerking gleefully, having fun while doing so. It is what it is what it is.

But embracing ho, embracing thot, embracing slut does not magically erase the historical degradation that these words are tied to in certain contexts. The embrace, however, does subvert the history, complicate it, and that's something. Because words like thot and ho are not just gendered slurs, they stand at the intersection of class and race, too, steeped in a kind of respectability that, when weaponized, equates "thotiness" with ratchetness,

ratchetness with ghettoness, ghettoness with poverty, poverty with inferiority. Respectability has always been a factor when it comes to Black women and their bodies; your hair, the way you speak, the way you dress, your size, the darkness or lightness of your skin have become tools with which to quantify a certain value or level of class.

Rapper The Game (a former spokesmodel for Fashion Nova Men, the opposite of luxury, mind you) has a song called "T.H.O.T." in which he shadily describes the woman of the title as "a Coach bag bitch but she follow Chanel." The insinuation is that everything about these women, including their bodies, is cheap. He raps in another line in the song about how he's going to "expose these bitches for who they are," thus exposing the ways in which specific words are weaponized against Black women.

Black women leading full and sexually fulfilling lives angers people enough for them to feel the need to police Black women's bodies. The women whom these words are aimed at are reclaiming the idea of being a thot or a ho; this makes some people uneasy because it shifts the power balance. And let's be clear—it's not just cis hetero men who are uneasy. Some women, too, have swallowed the seeds of misogyny and seek a kind of validation through the invalidation of other women's choices. That's what makes the idea of restructuring how that word lives and breathes in the language exciting, even if imperfect.

This unease with Black women having agency over their own bodies and sexualities is on display in online discourse about highly visible young Black women whose sexual lives seem to provide constant fodder for heated debate. In January 2020, Chloe, one-half of the singing duo Chloe x Halle, cried on her Instagram Live while discussing the criticism and harassment she had received for posting sexy photos and videos of herself on social media. "It's really hard for me to think of myself as a sexual being or attractive being," she said. "So, when I see all the uproar about my posts and stuff, I'm a bit confused . . . I don't post what I post to get attention." The fact that Chloe, a then-twenty-two-year-old girl just trying to explore her sensuality and love her body felt the need to give any explanation at all is aggravating and exhausting.

Equally exhausting are the numerous bad takes on Lori Harvey, the twenty-four-year-old daughter of Steve Harvey who garnered online attention simply for minding her business and dating several high-profile men, including Future, Trey Songz, Lewis Hamilton, and, allegedly, both Diddy and his son Christian Combs. Her dating history became a meme throughout 2019 and 2020, culminating with her going Instagram official with new boyfriend Michael B. Jordan in January 2021. To many people this was the ultimate upgrade, a supreme flex. And then there were those who saw the very public trajectory of Lori's dating life (which she herself has never publicly commented on) as everything wrong with Black women today.

In February 2021 thirty-eight-year-old rapper Boosie Badazz did an interview with Vlad TV in which he said he would never marry Lori Harvey (as if he'd ever have that option) because of her "high body count." Later, in a video posted on Instagram, he defended his comments:

> I wake up to all these Lori Harvey fans on my ass, talking about I'm hating on Lori. I just said y'all got it fucked up saying that's goals. If you saying that's goals that means you want your daughter to fuck seven or eight or nine niggas in a couple months in the industry. If that's cool, if that's goals for you, for your daughter doing that, then I can't say shit. But what's wrong with y'all motherfuckers is y'all salute the ones that get passed around. But y'all dog the women that stick by they nigga when they nigga fuck over. Y'all dog the real bitches who stick by they nigga, but y'all salute the bitches who go from hand to hand.

Why a man who bragged about allegedly paying an adult sex worker to perform oral sex on his underage pre-teen son and nephews thinks he has any legitimacy to question what people want for their daughters is unclear. What is clear is that Boosie's opinion is not an anomaly, and this preoccupation with policing young Black women's sexuality is ubiquitous and harmful in too many ways to mention. These critiques are presented with some sense of concern about the well-being or reputation of Black girls, but in actuality are very uninterested in these things. The fear isn't about the girl being "ran through" but the insecurity and lack of power that her sexual autonomy creates in the minds of men. So when T.I., for instance, publicly boasts about making sure his eighteen-year-old daughter's hymen is intact during visits to the gynecologist, he's not thinking about how potentially embarrassing or traumatizing his divulging that information is to her. He's merely thinking about himself.

The manner in which men (and indoctrinated women) engage with Black women's sexuality creates a false binary that mimics that of the virgin and the whore. This is why I've never been crazy about the word "Queen," how it's often used to police Black women's bodies by reminding them that they are too regal and too precious to fuck. It's all so steeped in the politics of respectability, in the myth that creates a demarcation between the values of so-called royalty and the low class. For one Black woman to be a queen, another has to be a ho, as if both identities could never exist in one being. Black women, even as we imagine new worlds where we get to take ownership of our bodies, are still vulnerable to the internalization of this false dichotomy. Indeed, Black women themselves can embrace and uphold many Hotep and Hotep-adjacent ideologies. A lot of times, I believe this internalization of misogyny is a kind of coping mechanism, a survival tool, a way to shield the body from violence by enacting that violence on others. A lot of times, it's so subtle that we don't even realize we're doing it.

Megan Thee Stallion, the twenty-six-year-old Houston, Texas, rapper, inspired an entire "hot girl summer" movement thanks to her feisty, fun, and raunchy lyrics. In 2020 Megan had been linked to several male artists, including Moneybagg Yo, G-Eazy, and Trey Songz—each rumored romance circulating in all the major Black gossip blogs, generating a narrative that she was "for the streets." In 2018, two years before her major success with her breakout single, "Savage," she gave an interview in which she talked about how she regularly sleeps with her exes in order to keep her "body count" low.

"Even if we break up, I'm still trying to fuck on you because I'm not adding no unnecessary shit," she explained on Hot 97's *Ebro in the Morning* show. "Do you know how long it took for us to do it? So like, hell no, we finna still do it. I can't. All that mileage, no. I ain't tryna run it up like that."

When the interview surfaced as Megan's star rose, I noticed several people on social media lamenting the fact that even Hot Girl Meg was susceptible to the policing of Black women's bodies, to the point where she would actively and proudly police her own. On the one hand, her statement could be seen as an explanation of why it's easier to return to an ex rather than go through the process of breaking in a new partner. On the other hand, "all that mileage" suggests a negative connotation with having numerous sexual partners. Of course, how Megan wants to navigate her "body count," whom she sleeps with and when, is solely up to her. There's a tendency to police the individual choices Black women make about their bodies that doesn't always make me feel comfortable, particularly in the moments when it's Black women who are doing the policing.

What Megan said in the interview stemmed from something so ubiquitous, after all, so human. It speaks to the deep and tangled roots of shame that run beneath our feet, periodically tripping us up even as we strive to do more, do better. Part of this lies in the fact that, outside of music, there have historically been fewer instances in pop culture in which we get to see Black women and girls explore their sexuality without shame or stigma as part of the narrative.

Hip-hop has long been a space for Black women artists to be unapologetic about their bodies and their sexuality. Women like Salt-N-Pepa, TLC, Lil' Kim, Foxy Brown, Nicki Minaj, Doja Cat, Mulatto, Saweetie, Kash Doll, Flo Milli, and Megan Thee Stallion have and are contributing to an ongoing archive of sexual autonomy in music. But even with strides toward expansiveness in terms of how Black women are allowed to express themselves, there is still a sense of boxing in, parameters and guidelines.

The twenty-nine-year-old Brooklyn rapper Young M.A has carved a niche for herself in the male-dominated rap game, where women rappers, no matter how good, are judged more intensely on their looks and heteronormative sex appeal. M.A, on the other hand, is masc, not femme, lesbian, not straight. Her sexually explicit lyrics (which of course are by no means free of the swaggering misogyny seen in the rhymes of her cis male counterparts) complicate and challenge expectations of who Black women rappers are performing their sexuality *for*, a question that inevitably comes up. If a Black woman isn't directing her sexuality at men, is it still worthy of attention? Is it still worthy of validation? Is it still worthy of respect? And what would the world look like if Black women claiming and reclaiming their sexuality wasn't seen solely as a performance but simply as an act of self-actualization and self-expression?

During a discussion at The New School in 2014, in reaction to Nicki Minaj's song "Anaconda" and its accompanying video, Black feminist thinker bell hooks said: "This shit is boring. What does it mean? Is there something missing that's happening here?" To hooks, there was nothing necessarily empowering about what Nicki was doing in the "Anaconda" video, where she and several other Black women writhe seductively in a jungle setting, their asses on full and proud display.

To hooks, Minaj's entire persona merely echoes images that perpetuate and denigrate Black women. hooks' skepticism seems to ask whether a Black woman's body and sexuality, packaged and commodified in this way, is truly tantamount to freedom. Minaj may be creating access and freedom for herself, but in doing so, is she upholding a patriarchal and racist structure that historically has always viewed Black women as commodities and nothing more? When can Black women take ownership of their sexualities, of their *bodies*, without it being a reflection of the desires of someone else—a person, a community, a society, whatever?

And it always boils down to bodies. The "value" we unknowingly and knowingly confer onto those bodies. Consider the 2020 banger "WAP" (Wet Ass Pussy) by Cardi B and Megan Thee Stallion. A sexual anthem all about two Black women's sexual prowess, in which Meg confidently spits, "I tell him where to put it, never tell him where I'm 'bout to be, I run down on him 'fore I have a nigga running me." This was the song of the summer. The song of the summer, I think, is there to tell us something implicit about the time in which it was written. With "WAP," what was perhaps most striking about it was the varying reactions to it, ranging from enthusiasm to downright outrage.

There was an interview I saw in *Far Out* magazine where CeeLo Green shared a sentiment echoed by many men (and women) after the song's release: "A lot of music today is very unfortunate and disappointing on a personal and moral level. There was once a time when we were savvy enough to code certain things. We could express to those it was meant for with the style of language we used. But now music is shameless, it is sheer savagery."

This from a man who was accused of rape in 2012. This from the man who defended himself by insisting it's only rape if the person is conscious. This from a man who recorded a song called "Necromancer" about fucking a dead woman. I recall reading the interview and wondering why Green was intentionally disregarding the long and rich history of Black women being outspoken and unapologetic about their sexuality in music, from Bessie Smith singing in 1923 "I need a little sugar in my bowl, I need a little hot dog on my roll" to Betty Davis singing in 1974 "He was a big freak, I used to beat him with a turquoise chain." Not to mention the sexually explicit lyrics of hip-hop juggernauts of the '80s and '90s, including the aforementioned Salt-N-Pepa, Lil' Kim, and Foxy Brown.

But this historical context is not as important as the need to dismiss the Black woman's sexual and artistic expression as "shameless," to reestablish the idea that a Black woman proudly proclaiming her sexual prowess, reveling in the pleasure *she* finds in her own body, is taboo, inappropriate, degrading. "WAP" came out just weeks after Megan Thee Stallion was shot in both her feet by rapper Tory Lanez, an incident that many on the internet regarded as a joke. There were memes about it, and some people even questioned/denied that Meg was really shot, prompting the young Houston rapper to post a picture of her wounds on Instagram to silence the skeptics.

On Twitter, Megan said: "Black women are so unprotected & we hold so many things in to protect the feelings of others w/o considering our own. It might be funny to y'all on the internet and just another messy topic for you to talk about but this is my real life and I'm real life hurt and traumatized."

I need you to understand that there is a connection, a tenuous thread, that connects the lack of care for Meg's body (and thus her life) after her traumatic and violent attack to the shaming, blaming, and outrage over her body as a prism through which she expresses her sexuality. In the often toxic, abusive comments section of gossip website The Shade Room, one can find observations about her that include: "She's built like a linebacker," and "That's a man." Curvy and 5'10" tall with brown skin, thick lips, a big nose, Meg is disrupting the idea of what kind of Black woman gets to be desirable, and desirous. In other words: her body is a threat and must therefore be dismantled and denigrated as a way to reinstate some kind of order.

She also forces uncomfortable questions to emerge, questions about what sorts of women and whats sorts of bodies *deserve* sympathy and support. There was a telling emergence of this dichotomy at the height of the popularity of "WAP" when, in September 2020, Tory Lanez produced a surprise album titled *Daystar* in which he tried to refute Megan's claims that he shot her or, at the very least, argue that there was more to the story. Some people wholeheartedly and enthusiastically supported Lanez's message. The outrage over Megan's explicit lyrics and the incredulity and disrespect launched at her by Lanez and his supporters were, in my mind, emergent symptoms of the same sickness.

It was the reaction to "WAP" and to the rise of Megan Thee Stallion that made me contemplate for the first time in a real way the connections between my own quiet hatred for my body, my sexual repression, and my sexual trauma. My teenage obsessions with wanting to be smaller, with wanting to look "done" at all times, with wanting my sensuality to fade into the background, were all a part of this need to be the "right" kind of Black woman and therefore more valuable and, ultimately, safe. Sex, then, and my own sexuality, was a mystery to me that I only received clues for when I was in my twenties, finally old enough to understand the ways in which society's disregard for my body had made *me* disregard my body and thus the potential for my own pleasure.

I've always been astounded at the ways in which art can reveal parts of ourselves and our stories to us long before we would have ever realized them on our own. I'm talking about the context and the specificity of time, how, for instance, a song can mean something entirely different to you at thirty-five than it did at fifteen.

For a long time, my earliest memory of sex, or rather of thinking about sex, was connected to a movie, *The Color Purple*, which I first saw when I was around seven or eight years old, long before I knew it was based on a book by Alice Walker. All my recollections of childhood are vague and a little hazy (a result of trauma, I've been told, go figure), but I do remember some feelings vividly.

I remember a queasiness in the pit of my stomach during the scene when Celie and Shug Avery talk one-on-one for the first time during Shug's visit. Celie, played so wonderfully by Whoopi Goldberg, explains to Shug the sad extent of her sex life. "He just climb on top of me and do his business," she says.

I remember the queasy feeling sort of intensifying, becoming a concentrated brick of uneasiness when Shug responds, "Do his business? You sound like he going to the toilet in you."

"That's what it feels like."

I remember feeling a wave of recognition that I didn't understand. I remember, too, the contrast to those emotions when I saw Shug and Celie kiss. Celie sits on the edge of a bed and lowers her eyes meekly as Shug (Margaret Avery) kisses her softly on the forehead, then on the cheek, then on the lips. I'd never seen two women kiss, let alone two Black women. I had the vaguest understanding of queerness, and whatever understanding I had of it had been shaped by religious adults who generally implied that it was bad.

But I recall such a lucid and specific thought for someone so young in watching the tenderness passed between Shug and Celie: sex, whatever this mysterious thing was, could be a good thing. A warming thing. A thing done with love. I would only realize years and years later what a tiny gift the memory of that feeling was, how it planted a seed of intuition inside me, of hope. Even though I had experienced a similar sexual trauma as Celie, a similar loss of control of my body, that didn't mean sex could or would never be a good thing again.

In 2011, Steven Spielberg, who controversially directed *The Color Purple* in 1985, admitted something I hadn't been aware of until I eventually read the Alice Walker novel in my teens.

"There were certain things in the relationship between Shug Avery and Celie that were finely detailed in Alice's book, that I didn't feel could get a [PG-13] rating and I was shy about it," Spielberg told *Entertainment Weekly*.

"In that sense, perhaps I was the wrong director to acquit some of the more sexually honest encounters . . . I basically took something that was extremely erotic and very intentional, and I reduced it to a simple kiss. I got a lot of criticism for that."

One might argue that at seven or eight, I probably had no business watching *The Color Purple* anyway. The kiss was enough of a revelation for me at that age, a kind of portal through which I could see, finally, Black women expressing their sexuality on screen in a way that felt loving and, most of all, affirming. Still, I have often thought about Spielberg's admitted timidity (cowardice might even be the word) when it came to depicting Black women's, especially Black lesbians', sexuality on screen. What was it about the honesty of the scene that made him shy? Was it a lack of concern? Or, worse, a lack of imagination when it came to conceiving of two Black women loving one another? Probably a little of all three, which is frustrating, given the fact that filmmakers and showrunners and executives have historically seemed to have a far more robust capacity for imagination when it comes to white women and their sex lives.

This isn't to say that there are *no* depictions of Black women enjoying vibrant, fully realized, complicated, and real sex lives in mainstream pop culture (*Insecure* is obviously the biggest contender in this category at the moment). There is always *some* kind of depiction of the thing you want to see represented if you look hard enough, I suppose. But the fact that you have to look hard at all is, to my mind, a problem. Greater access to these depictions, these images, is critical.

But I know that for every ridiculous video objectifying Black women's bodies, like Taylor Swift's video for "Shake It Off," in which the Black female body is played as novelty, a literal booty-poppin' prop for Swift to poke her head through, I'm reminded of videos like City Girls' "Twerk," in which dozens of Black women were "flewed out" to joyously shake their asses with not a man in sight, and in the end one lucky lady wins money for her moves.

Images like this, of Black women being joyful and unafraid of the sexual power of their bodies, are vital. And when I say "vital" I mean this sincerely and not as some empty platitude. When you consider the fact that Black women were once young Black girls, many of whom were socialized to hide their bodies, to not engage with them in a meaningful way, to obscure their bodies from the eyes of stepfathers and uncles and cousins and brothers, to shrink themselves in order to live, the vitality of these images becomes all the more clear. The sexuality and body consciousness of Black women are formed early on. Watching *The Color Purple* planted a seed in me that was only allowed to blossom later; the long delay was mostly because I was offered so few glimpses of Black women experiencing their bodies from a place of joy.

There's a reason why I didn't have any positive meaningful sexual experiences until well into my twenties. I didn't have the spiritual language for it. I don't blame this solely on movies, or TV shows, my upbringing, or even my abuser. I know that rather all of these things coalesced to create that silence, conspiring together to ensure that I would not develop a language for my sexuality that wasn't contingent on what other people felt about it. I could not desire because I believed I was inherently undesirable. Repressed sexual trauma took up any remaining space I needed to enjoy my body on my own terms.

When the documentary *Surviving R. Kelly* came out in early 2019, opinions were divided: for every horrified reaction to the allegations of sexual abuse and predatory behavior on the part of Kelly, there was also skepticism and even blame toward his young female victims, most under-age when they became involved with Kelly. It is the kind of criticism that plays right into an American historical narrative about young Black women: that they were "fast," that they were consenting, even though they were minors and their sexuality should have been off limits to any adult.

Roxane Gay said out loud what we all were thinking in an online interview with Vox Media in February. She declared:

> We see it all the time with Black girls and women where we're not allowed our childhoods, we're not allowed innocence, we're not allowed the benefit of the doubt. I think that our bodies from a very young age are over-policed and of course over-sexualized. And that's why we see a lack of empathy for Black girls who have been lured into R. Kelly's cult. And we're told, "Oh you should have known better." Or, "She was acting fast." And, no, she was a child who was being preyed upon by a known predator. And very few people did anything to protect them. And are still, frankly, doing very little to protect them, because he's still not behind bars. And I assure you that if R. Kelly was preying upon young white girls, they would have built a prison on top of him.

A year later, one of Kelly's victims, Azriel Clary, who met the predator when she was only seventeen, became fodder for the online gossip mill when she took to social media to reveal some of her story. She posted Instagram Lives of herself verbally arguing with Kelly's girlfriends, and another video in which she insisted that Aaliyah wasn't the first of R. Kelly's underage girlfriends.

"I am not the first person this man has done this to," the then-twenty-three-year-old said in a video posted in April 2020. "This has been happening since the nineties. This has been happening since way before Aaliyah."

Her videos were screen-recorded and re-shared on sites like Bossip and The Shade Room, where for every comment expressing compassion, there were a dozen essentially blaming her for being groomed, manipulated, brainwashed, and abused, and another dozen accusing her of "clout chasing" and gold digging.

There is something so specifically painful, and recognizable, in the spectacle of her pain, the memefication and virality of her experience. Clary said she was sharing her story publicly in an effort to heal. Her healing, much like her actual abuse, became an afterthought, secondary to the act of judging her, defining her, impeding her ability to reclaim her own narrative.

Reclaiming narratives around our bodies and reclaiming and owning the language and words we use to describe our own bodies is a kind of alchemy. But how can you reclaim something that you cannot even name? For years I never fully grasped that we hold on to memories and hold on to traumas long after we've experienced them and felt them, deep in our flesh and our bones. We dissociate during sex, or have panic attacks when someone touches us the wrong way, or lean into reckless hyper-sexuality and mistake that for autonomy, or deny ourselves sexual pleasure and mistake that for discipline.

If you asked me to tell you the specific history of trauma etched into my body, I wouldn't be able to. There is a chasm where my past should be. I have little memory of *it,* but I can feel *it.* A violation that you cannot articulate beyond general brushstrokes of pain is frustrating in so many ways, but perhaps most of all in the way that it makes you question your body, your mind, and the narrative of your own sexuality. Sexual assault victims are expected to know exactly what happened to them and how, to offer up a clear and uncomplicated portrait of their abuse, despite the havoc that trauma wreaks on our minds. For Black women especially, this delegitimization of our experiences shows up in the world in profound and tangible ways. The fact that one in four Black girls will be abused before the age of eighteen, that one in five Black women are survivors of rape, and yet for every fifteen Black women who are assaulted just one reports her rape comes as no surprise. I imagine we are less likely to report our abuse because we feel we are less likely to be believed, to be held.

These connections between knowing and not knowing, the inheritance of sexual trauma, and the repression of pain are visceral and real and ever present for so many of us. All of these histories are etched into our bodies, and we often carry them without even fully understanding these histories.

In all of this I think of Sarah Baartman, whose story you probably know even if you do not know her name. She was a South African woman who was exhibited as a freak show attraction to white audiences across Europe in the nineteenth century. I think of how she was dubbed by whites as the "Hottentot Venus." I think of how, after she died, her genitals were preserved in a jar of formaldehyde and put on display.

I think about The Carters' song "Black Effect," the part where Beyoncé proudly sings about her "Sarah Baartman hips," how her booty is so fat she has to jump to get into her jeans. I think about how surreal and how sad, how full circle that is. In referencing Sarah Baartman, I wonder, is Beyoncé reclaiming and reframing her tragic narrative? Or is she merely further, in a sense, commodifying her image? Can both of these things be true at once?

Here's the thing about reclaiming these words and reclaiming these bodies, our bodies: it isn't easy. It isn't simple. It doesn't mean that the words we redefine can't and won't continue to be weaponized against us. This is a reality, but one, I think, that exists in tandem with an equally potent reality: that Black women have the power to define and redefine who they are, always and forever. The thing I love about definitions is that they are not static things, they constantly shift, change, take on new meanings.

A while back, while scrolling through Twitter, I came

across a meme someone had posted, pink words against a white background. It read "I'm a THOT. Trustworthy, honest, outgoing, thoughtful." I read it, and chuckled, and marveled at how a word can mean so many things at once.

Claudette Colvin

Claudette Colvin, age 13, in 1953. The Visibility Project.

Man, This Shit Is Draining

The most unpleasant experiences I've had on the internet have always been tied to race. When you write about race for a major news publication, racist white people often feel obligated to be indignant about it. It's as if they see it as a duty to be outraged. Also cruel. Writing about the realities of this country—that it was built on the exploitation and death of Black and Indigenous people, that it has yet to fully reckon with this—seems to incense the type of people who feel that they are entitled to express their rage whenever, wherever, however, and to whomever they want, including virtual strangers.

In May 2020 I published a *HuffPost* piece called "Amy Cooper Knew Exactly What She Was Doing," about an incident in which a white woman in Central Park called the police in hysterics when a Black man calmly reminded her that her dog was not allowed off the leash in that section of the park. In the piece I wrote that white people, even those who believe they hold no power or biases, must unpack the fact that "They are complicit—and even participatory—in the system of white supremacy."

The thing I've learned about a lot of racists over the last ten-plus years of writing online is that as obsessed as they are with race, many of them don't have the range to actually discuss it, to fully understand the nuance and the truth of my statement. And so, instead of meaningful engagement with my work, I received dozens of angry correction emails calling me all types of racial and gendered slurs. For example, from fuckyou@___.com, with the subject heading "Fuck you": "All whites are white supremacists? Not exactly how you get people on your side, nigger."

And another email from a reader calling himself "Vlad," this one in response to a piece I had written about the myth of reverse racism: "I suggest this nigger whore Zeba Blay go fuck herself."

And from someone named S.J.:

> I really liked this article's point until you decided to be a racist bitch about it, so hey, i'll have you know

i admit exactly how much i am aware of racism as a systemic, structural evil oppressing the disenfranchised and voiding the very concept of democratic representation. so go fuck yourself for branding me "white" and writing me off you vile cunt.

I've gotten emails sent to me with subject headings like "How Can You Call Yourself a Film Critic?" for pointing out that a movie (the abysmal, inexplicably Oscar-winning *Green Book*) was racially unaware. Other emails have contained nothing but the word *nigger* typed hundreds of times. I've had people encourage me to kill myself, on days when I've actually wanted to kill myself. Once, also in response to a piece on reverse racism, someone sent a picture to my personal email account of my face photoshopped onto the body of a lynched woman hanging from a bridge. Sometimes I wish I hadn't immediately deleted it, just to serve as a record, just to validate the experience (which I was accused of lying about when I mentioned it on Twitter), but honestly, it was one of the most traumatizing things I've ever seen.

Welcome to being a Black woman on the internet. Welcome to being harassed online, and sometimes in person, and having no recourse for dealing with the bullshit. Welcome to rarely reporting trolls and abusers on social media because you've already resigned yourself to the fact that these billion-dollar platforms ultimately do not give a fuck about you. Welcome to friends and family lovingly but naively telling you that this is just "part of the job" and "if you don't have haters you're doing something wrong." Welcome to convincing yourself that the harassment is normal, a fact of life, just for the sake of being able to go on. Welcome to stemming your anger, hurt, and disillusionment because to do the opposite would mean to simply invite more of the same abuse. Welcome to being mad.

In *Sister Outsider*, Audre Lorde speaks of how "every Black woman in America lives her life somewhere along a wide curve of ancient and unexpressed angers." Our anger runs deep. We have an intimate understanding of the many shades of anger. It isn't always red hot. Sometimes it's bright white and cool to the touch. It glows and grows, slowly, consistently, until one day when it's pitch black, blacker than black, swallowing you up and any person, place, or thing that gets in your way. These are the moments when you say fuck it, the moments where you go off on the passive-aggressive white girl at your job, or embark upon a long, tenuous rant toward some ain't shit dude in your life, or, in the boldest of caps lock, post a tirade about the latest brown or Black body slain by police on your Twitter feed. Your anger can be epic, it can be banal, but when it's over, the reaction invariably is: "Calm down."

There is freedom in displaying anger, in not being calm. There is a freedom in the entitlement that comes with sending emails and tweets and Instagram DMs berating strangers on the internet (something I have never even considered let alone wanted to do). There is freedom

in white male rage, in for instance the ability say whatever you want on Twitter with tirades and temper tan-
trums and calls for violence and insurrection on a whim
for four years, silenced only at the last possible minute,
when the chaos of your ego has already done its dam-
age (I am talking about Trump). There's freedom, too, in
white female anger, in the ability of white women's anger
to be viewed as righteous and true, to be politicized, to
be weaponized when asking to "speak to the manager,"
when accusing a Black boy of whistling, to inspire rage
in others through the use of pointed fingers and tears.
These freedoms are rarely afforded to Black women without complication.

After the chaotic 2020 U.S. presidential election, Michelle Obama made an Instagram post urging a peaceful
handoff of power from one old white man to another,
amid protests from Trump and his surrogates that the
election had been stolen from him. She wrote of her experience of welcoming Donald and Melania Trump to
the White House in 2017:

> I have to be honest and say that none of this was
> easy for me. Donald Trump had spread racist lies
> about my husband that had put my family in danger.
> That wasn't something I was ready to forgive. But I
> knew that, for the sake of our country, I had to find
> the strength and maturity to put my anger aside. So
> I welcomed Melania Trump into the White House

and talked with her about my experience, answering every question she had—from the heightened scrutiny that comes with being First Lady to what it's like to raise kids in the White House . . . I knew in my heart it was the right thing to do, because our democracy is so much bigger than anybody's ego.

There was something so incredibly painful about reading those words, something painful in considering the psychic toll that "when they go low, we go high" truly takes. I believe that for Black women, anger is a precarious state of being, an emotion that requires calculation and compromise and bravery to express. We must dig deep, so often, to quell it. When we do express anger, we open ourselves up to ridicule, dismissal, tone-policing, violence. This violence can take on many forms. Sometimes it manifests in words, threats, slurs, rude gestures. Other times it's deeper than that.

When I'm angry in public spaces, especially spaces dominated by figures of authority, what flashes in my brain are the names and faces of Sandra Bland and Korryn Gaines, Black women who lost their lives in the direct aftermath of their anger. The video of Sandra Bland's traffic stop replays in my mind, her justified annoyance and exasperation a kind of omen. I can see Korryn Gaines' standoff with police, and I get chills thinking about the fact that in these moments, these women have only hours, minutes left to live.

These are women who, even in death, were criticized

for failing to remain calm in situations where anyone else would have been the opposite. The criticism, seen in news headlines and social media comments, is always the same: by falling into their anger, they fell into a trap, they played into a stereotype, they validated it, and thus, implicitly, they deserved what they got.

Oversimplifications haunt Black women. One of the most persistent specters is that of the Angry Black Woman. She is not real, she is imagined, and yet we see her in every nook and cranny of the culture, in our movies and TV shows, in the real world. We see her on reality television, pushed to an orchestrated boiling point and then vilified for doing so. We see her when sports journalist Jemele Hill raises her voice and speaks her mind about Donald Trump's racist rhetoric and loses her job for it. We see her when Michelle Obama rolls her eyes or doesn't smile and is deemed the most disrespectful first lady in history by the right-wing press. We see her when Congresswoman Maxine Waters is met with vitriol and hate for outspokenly calling for people to challenge politicians who sanction and support placing immigrant children in cages.

You must remember this. In 2018, in response to news of immigrant families being torn apart by ICE, Congresswoman Waters said: "We're going to win this battle . . . Let's make sure we show up wherever we have to show up. And if you see anybody from that Cabinet in a restaurant, in a department store, at a gasoline station, you get out and you create a crowd and you push back on them and you tell them they're not welcome."

This statement, a simple rallying cry for people to use words to express their dissatisfaction with their government, led to Waters being met with slurs and death threats (of shooting, lynching, beating), and Democratic leaders like Speaker of the House Nancy Pelosi and Senator Chuck Schumer distancing themselves from her as much as possible. Schumer described her words as "not American." President Trump, unsurprisingly, described her as crazy, defined her rallying cry as nothing more than "ranting and raving." The consensus was that she was doing too much and that she should shut up.

This episode wasn't the first nor the last time Waters had been painted as a threat, as too aggressive, as too opinionated. It was part of an ongoing cycle: the Angry Black Woman trope at work. It is, at its core, a silencing tactic. Waters, now in her eighties, has spent her life advocating for peaceful protest and change, but the Angry Black Woman trope, in one fell swoop, is continually used to depict her as someone, or rather something, to be feared, or not to be taken seriously. This is how this stereotype has worked against Black women for centuries. It makes one wonder whether it's ever really worth it to be peaceful, if even that approach is liable to be misconstrued and vilified.

In her book *Eloquent Rage*, Brittney Cooper writes about a simple truth. That truth being that "Angry Black Women are looked upon as entities to be contained, as inconvenient citizens who keep on talking about their rights while refusing to do their duty and smile at everyone."

The concept of Black women as "inconvenient citizens" encapsulates everything that fuels this trope to this day. The Angry Black Woman is inconveniently loud, inconveniently aggressive. She is quick to pop off, almost delusional in her rage, in a constant state of hostility, easily provoked, and even more easily ignored. The stereotype, like so many negative stereotypes about Black women, began in the Jim Crow era, in the minstrel era, in the time when ideas about Black people fostered by white people first began entering the culture as a whole.

The first iteration of the Angry Black Woman came in the form of the Mammy figure, with her fiery one-liners, lambasting her husband and children or sassing her white employers (during Jim Crow, it was illegal for Black people to argue with whites, so the idea of the Mammy figure talking back to white people was inherently absurd and thus hilarious to white folk). Her impertinence was seen as tied to the very nature of Black womanhood, but she was always ultimately loyal to the white status quo and thus her anger was never really taken that seriously.

Through minstrelsy, through vaudeville, through the movies of the 1920s and '30s with their stock Mammy characters, the seeds of the Angry Black Woman trope were sown and began to grow. They would bloom with the character of Sapphire Stevens. Sapphire was introduced to the zeitgeist through the popular radio and then television program *Amos 'n' Andy*, about two Black best friends (played by white men on the radio series) whittled down to bumbling caricatures of Black manhood.

Sapphire Stevens was the shrew-like wife of one of the show's lead characters, and her chief duty was to be a figure of constant antagonism. She berated her husband, flew into rages, and seemed to exist in a near-perpetual state of dissatisfaction. As a character in one of the most popular sitcoms of the twentieth century, she set the tone for how Black women, especially dark-skinned Black women, especially in comedy, would continue to be portrayed to white and Black audiences alike.

Sapphire begat many daughters. Some of them, it must be acknowledged, were and are beloved even as they play into or with the Angry Black Woman stereotype. Women like Pam on *Martin* (not to mention the caricature of Sheneneh), Tyler Perry's creation Madea, Cookie Lyon on *Empire*, Tara Thornton on *True Blood*, Florence Johnston on *The Jeffersons*, nearly every Black female cast member on reality TV, Minny Jackson in *The Help*. Some of these characters are fully realized human beings, others are distilled down to the lowest common denominator of their anger. But, generally speaking, their anger is presented as something that makes them figures of fun or entertainment or stimulation. When a Black woman passionately voicing an opinion or expressing anger is met with a laugh track, it echoes if not fully embraces caricatures of long ago.

That's not to say that there isn't value in some of these

characters. I've always felt that seeing a Black woman fully embrace and express her anger can be a good thing, an important thing. Just because the Angry Black Woman stereotype has tainted depictions of Black women on screen in the past doesn't mean that in order to combat it we pretend that Black women never get angry or sassy at all. That wouldn't be real life. And sometimes, the results are transcendent. Think of Angela Bassett in *Waiting to Exhale* as she stares at an endless sea of her ain't shit husband's shoes and clothes, meticulously organized, and then throws them all into a car that she sets on fire as she bellows, "Get your shit, get your shit, and get out!" It's not a caricature, it's catharsis. The flames fill up the background, and she walks toward the camera, her face etched with righteous anger, her hair gloriously laid.

The problem is that the caricatures live on, even as we try to subvert them. In a cartoon published in Australia's *Herald Sun* on September 10, 2018, illustrator Mark Knight depicted Serena Williams during the finals match at the U.S. Open Tennis Championships as a classic racist caricature. In the foreground, he sketched her as a looming, Hulk-like figure with unkempt hair and cartoonishly large lips jumping up and down, mid-tantrum, a broken racket beneath her feet.

In the background, Knight drew Williams' competitor, the half-Black half-Japanese Naomi Osaka. Osaka's appearance had been distilled down to its lowest-common-denominator characteristics: light skin, slim frame, blond hair. She might as well have been Maria Sharapova. Her whitewashed figure peers up at an umpire, who says, in a dialogue bubble, "Can you just let her win?"

Caricatures, by their nature, are meant to distort and exaggerate. But they're also meant to be symbolic, representative, shorthand for a concept or idea. Here, the narrative was clear: Williams had been cast as the big, ugly, Angry Black Woman. Osaka, by contrast, had been cast as the innocent white girl, even though she's not even white.

The cartoon was just part of the fallout stemming from Williams' infamous U.S Open match against Osaka, where she broke her racket in frustration, where she reprimanded the umpire for insinuating that she cheated, where she asked him, several times, for a formal apology. For this, she was fined $17,000.

The fine and the reactions to Williams' behavior, especially in contrast to Osaka's behavior, were in keeping with a consistent and collective inability in the culture to see Black women as complex and capable of expressing a myriad of emotions, from rage to joy to despair. Or to allow two Black women to reach for excellence at the same time.

Williams apparently struggled with her behavior during the match, writing later in an essay for *Harper's BAZAAR* that she started to see a therapist and could not even bring herself to pick up a tennis racket for several days after she played Osaka. She wrote an apology letter to Osaka, which read:

As I said on the court, I am so proud of you and I am truly sorry. I thought I was doing the right thing in sticking up for myself. But I had no idea the media would pit us against each other. I would love the chance to live that moment over again. I am, was, and will always be happy for you and supportive of you. I would never, ever want the light to shine away from another female, specifically another black female athlete. I can't wait for your future, and believe me I will always be watching as a big fan! I wish you only success today and in the future. Once again, I am so proud of you.

All my love and your fan, Serena.

Osaka replied, according to Williams, by saying that "People can misunderstand anger for strength because they can't differentiate between the two . . . No one has stood up for themselves the way you have and you need to continue trailblazing."

The grace, the understanding that Black women can extend to one another even in moments of seeming conflict, is profound. That Williams had to wrestle with these feelings at all, though, is a testament to the ways in which misogynoir, particularly against dark-skinned Black women, can burrow into the mind and find a home.

Two years after her 2018 match with Williams, Osaka would throw her own racket in frustration during a U.S. Open match against Marta Kostyuk. This gesture, similar to Williams', would garner headlines like "Frustrated Naomi Osaka survives to reach US Open Round of 16" (from the *New York Post*) and "Osaka tosses racket, overcomes test from teenager at US Open" from an article in the AP, in which writer Howard Fendrich wrote understandingly: "Sometimes, that's the sort of reaction it takes to right things for Osaka."

What an obvious and predictable contrast to headlines after the Osaka-Williams match: "Serena Williams' temper is building ugly US Open legacy" (this piece was by Marc Berman, the same *New York Post* journalist who who wrote the empathetic Naomi Osaka article referenced above).

These headlines, and Knight's cartoon, shine a light on what happens when we flatten human beings into types, when the story and its narrative become far more important than the nuance of the situation. In the process, racist and sexist assumptions are perpetuated, and we strip people of their right to be weak *and* strong, angry *and* calm. We strip them of the totality of their humanity. And yet, of course, it seems that only Black women are paying attention to this. I can't imagine being extended the kind of grace and spaciousness to express my anger in my own professional world, which exists on this page and also online, in the way that Osaka and Williams did for each other behind the scenes. I can't imagine my humanity being regarded as anything other than irrelevant.

Humanity is a word and a concept that comes up over and over again for me whenever I feel trapped in a haze of online harassment. I often wonder, where exactly is the humanity in this person trolling me? And when I ask that question, it's not in reference to the good and kind aspects of their personality. I believe that seeing humanity in a person doesn't necessarily mean seeing their innate goodness. Instead, it simply means acknowledging that this is a whole person having a whole human experience. Taking that into consideration modifies the way you interact with people, the way you experience people. I understand a tenet of racist thinking is to deny the humanity of Black people and yet, still, witnessing and living the reality of that is far more disruptive than grasping the concept.

My tactic for several years now has been to delete the message, the email, the tweet, before I even get the chance to read it. I've gotten good at spotting trolls—usually, if it's a Twitter profile, they have no profile pic, a wack ass, generic username, and zero followers. It's clear that a lot of these accounts have been created to specifically and intentionally harass me. I see them, I mute them, I tell myself, "I will not feed this monster. I will not dignify this with a response." Which is so, so hard. Which makes me angry.

I think the thing that makes me angriest is being willfully misunderstood, and my personhood being sidelined and dismissed in order to fit neatly into a stranger's narrative of the world. In this scenario, instead of a fully realized person—stubborn, curious, anxious, hurting, healing, shady, insecure, generous, well-meaning, funny, a little empty—I'm flattened into the member of some opposing team: the Blacks, the Libs, SJWs.

People who treat actual life as though it were a football game where your only choice is to root for a specific team baffle me. People who expect you to give them grace but offer no grace to you in return, truthfully, scare me. But again, most of all, there's an ugliness to this behavior that just makes me so unbelievably mad. I deeply resent the fact that the internet is not a real place, and yet it dictates so much of our reality.

These trolls and harassers, usually white, almost always white cis heterosexual men, don't care about this impact on the real world and real life, because life to them is an abstract concept. They love to play devil's advocate, as if the devil doesn't already have enough advocates. Debating the oppression of other people is a game of hypotheticals to them, and they see racism as a speculative concept rather than a true lived experience. They find genuine happiness and content in exhausting and dehumanizing the Black and brown strangers whom they target online. They are, as Toni Morrison once said of racists, utterly bereft. It is too much of a psychic toll to engage with these kinds of people.

I often wonder if my inclination to disengage comes from that fear of my anger being "inconvenient" or, better yet, dismissed. Feeding into exactly what is expected of me. But there's something else at play. These online harassers are like gnats, really. More annoying than anything else, but when you're bugged enough times annoyance can churn itself into rage. The fear is that giving in to that rage is giving them what they want: the sensation of me taking any of the bullshit they have to say seriously, which I don't. This is the conundrum.

Because there's another part of me that *just wants to destroy*. To rage. To poke fine, deliberate holes into every gripe they have, to rub their faces in the fact that the only reason they read my articles and then seek me out to rudely complain about them is because (a) they're racist and (b) they can't take the idea of me having carved out a real platform on the internet that's not merely a Twitter feed where I berate people as a way to cope with emptiness and purposelessness. There's a part of me that does want to go back and forth, purely for my own satisfaction. This urge builds up and up and up. I know myself. I'll never engage. But, unlike them, I have a book. So I'll allot this space to say:

Fuck you. Fuck your disingenuous attempts to debate me about my feelings. Fuck your complaining. Fuck your shitty hot takes. Fuck your emails, your tweets, your DMs, your useless corrections. Fuck your slurs, your racist memes. Fuck your extreme self-denial. Fuck your toxicity. Fuck your destructive insecurity. Fuck your performative racism, your pathetic bids to get attention via my shine. Fuck the several hours it took you to track me down on every social media platform that I occupy just to call me a nigger and tell me that I suck. Fuck you for thinking I care. Fuck your cruelty. Fuck your smallness. Fuck the banality of your existence. Fuck your violent threats. Fuck your judgment. Fuck you for thinking you can explain what being a Black woman is like to a fucking Black woman. Fuck you for your inability to cope with a Black woman having a platform, especially when you don't. Fuck you for your acute inability to think or talk about race in a nuanced and mature and honest way. Fuck your boring inability to engage with race on any level beyond feeling hurt and attacked when a Black person tells you what it feels like to be oppressed. Fuck your complete lack of self-awareness. Fuck trying to make you understand. Fuck a dialogue. Fuck being the bigger person. Fuck your entitlement to my energy and time. Fuck a back-and-forth conversation about some article I wrote five years ago and never think about. Fuck a heart-to-heart. Fuck you and your entire existence, completely. Grow up. Grow.

That was a release. That felt nice. But I'll be honest: the act of allotting a single paragraph in a book to my anger feels like a metaphor for how I, as a Black woman, have dealt with my anger for years. In little compartments, in little outbursts. I have volumes of anger within me that language cannot contain. And yet I am, still, always concerned with keeping my voice even and my thoughts clear when I can see nothing but rage. Always keenly concerned about how the reverberations of my anger will bounce back on me. What reactions will I get? Will I, for once, be taken seriously? The innate worry that to express my anger is to expose myself not only to ridicule or dismissal but to disbelief clings to me.

What the Angry Black Woman myth erases: Black women are almost always *justified* in their anger. We don't need to prove anything to you. We don't need to pull out receipts or itemized lists. We don't need to explain in minute detail how we got from A to B. Our anger is enough. Believe us.

There is so much that I am mad about. Not just the abuse online, not just the abuse I've witnessed other Black women experience. Not just the double standards that the prominent Black women I've mentioned above have had to endure publicly. Not just the injustices and abuse and dismissal that the Black women and femmes I love have had to endure privately. I'm mad that, often, I don't know what to do with my anger at all. How to harness it. How to face it.

Something I'm trying to learn, to teach myself, is that my anger about the state of the world, about the state of my life and the lives of people close to me, can be what fuels me. It doesn't necessarily diminish me, as the caricatures and stereotypes would have me believe. Because something I'm sure of is that after rage comes serenity. The thing about anger is that it's all about release, about the expulsion of built-up emotional pressure. It's poison to keep that in. That's why they want us to, because it doesn't challenge them or their worldview. But we can find new ways of release, new ways of channeling. The point is, though, that we're allowed to let go.

What's key is to have instances where our anger is reflected back to us in affirming, validating ways. Not as punchlines, not as catalysts for tragic stories. I'd like to give a shout out to Solange Knowles at this moment—a woman whose unabashed anger has been well documented, gossiped about, nitpicked, memeified. She's provided one of those affirming, validating moments for Black women that I speak of.

Picture this: a Black woman (me) standing on her bed, eyes closed, arms wrapped around herself, head tilted to the side, crooning out the words "You've got a right to be mad," for the first time, in tandem with the voice of Solange, echoing throughout the room.

This is a moment I hold on to: the first time I heard that song, the first time I embraced that idea: *I have a right to be mad.* And not because anyone gave me permission to, but because I gave it to myself.

Cicely Tyson

Cicely Tyson in *The Autobiography of Miss Jane Pittman*, 1974.

Extra Black

There is no singular dark-skinned-girl experience, but if there is one constant to the journey, I imagine it's the striving to maintain a sense of oneself amid the projections of other people. Little assumptions and expectations about who you are and what you're worth are grafted onto your skin before you've even found the vocabulary to understand the meaning of your skin outside of a white supremacist context. How to get free of that?

Over a decade ago, when I was sixteen or seventeen, an older Black woman so light that I initially mistook her for white stopped me in the street as I was walking home from school. She needed to tell me, loudly and effusively and in the middle of the road, that I was beautiful. She made a big show of it, too, which made me, painfully awkward and insecure in a way so specific to being a teenage girl, mortified.

When you're sixteen years old, fully convinced that you are the ugliest person in the world, the idea of being told by random strangers that you are beautiful seems fantastic, but only in theory. For me, being complimented by a stranger was complicated by having to confront the fact that being told you are beautiful will never be the same as believing that you are beautiful. Instead, the woman's praise felt like some sort of test that I was failing, or a joke. It felt worse when she began to compliment my complexion.

"You have gorgeous skin, sweetie," she gushed. "Don't ever let anybody make you feel any different. Don't ever feel bad about that beautiful chocolate skin!" I managed a semblance of a smile and muttered a thank-you before power walking away. I knew then and now that she was well meaning, but I was not flattered. I was annoyed. I was annoyed at the idea of a compliment wrapped up in presumption. *"Don't ever feel bad about that beautiful chocolate skin!"*

That's always the assumption that's made about women with dark skin, isn't it? That we hate our skin. That we feel "bad" about it. That our skin is something we *should* feel bad about. And, what's more, the assumption places all the blame of our real or imagined traumas and insecurities and hang-ups on us, never once shifting focus to acknowledge that before we could hate our skin the world showed us how to. One way or another, colorism finds a way to infiltrate our image of ourselves.

I'm your average so-called chocolate complexioned girl, but I've never had any issues about my dark skin. I've wanted to be thinner, prettier, have a fatter ass and a complexion that wasn't acne prone, but I've never desperately wanted to be lighter than I am. Since going natural in my teens, I've struggled with figuring out how to care for my zig-zag kinky hair, but I've never wished my hair was straight. And yet I've always had terrible self-esteem. The story goes that dark girls with low self-esteem feel that way because they want to be something else. I never wanted to be something else, yet I always understood, intrinsically and from a young age, that maybe other people did.

Part of that understanding comes with a knowledge that however I personally feel about the color of my skin does not change the realities of what it's like to walk through this world as a dark-skinned Black woman with big lips and kinky hair and edges that don't lie down.

As a young girl, before I had even fully processed the concept of race and skin color, I understood that there were going to be people who saw my skin not only as undesirable but as a kind of liability. I'd been subtly indoctrinated to believe that there was a hierarchy to skin color that was pervasive and concrete, and we, as dark-skinned Black women, and girls especially, were at the very bottom of that hierarchy. This unspoken rule, this lie, seemed embedded in how I experienced the world from an early age. Sometimes the reality of colorism, of being discriminated against because I had darker skin, was so loud I could barely think. Other times, most times, it was quiet and subtle—so nearly imperceptible that I've had to second-guess myself about whether what I'm experiencing is a form of colorism at all, or just an echo of my own paranoia and self-doubt.

These moments may seem slight as they happen, but over time they pile up one on top of another into a giant mound of anxiety. Moments like when I was nine or ten at some summer camp in upstate New York for a school trip, and a Black boy from another school, a boy just as dark as me, called me an "ugly Black blob" outside the mess hall. I cried so hard that I burst a vessel in my eyeball.

When I was in my early twenties, hanging out in bars with my white or lighter-skinned Black girlfriends, a knot of apprehension would settle at my core, because I knew intuitively that only one of us was going to get hit on at the bar.

It wasn't as though I *wanted* to be hit on—male attention in those kinds of environments often feels like violence—but I was a young woman buckling under societal pressure and made to feel that if I was not drawing the attention of heterosexual cis men, even violent attention, then that said something about my worthiness. And so, to walk into those bars and accept almost as a matter of fact that my friend would get more attention merely because she was lighter than me hurt in a way that didn't register at the time. The pain was small and constant—an ache that I got used to and never made an effort to examine.

As a preteen, I looked at the light-skinned, curly haired Black and Afro-Latinx girls in my 7th and 8th grade classes, the popular girls who slicked down their baby hairs into dainty spirals and swoops and made a fuss whenever they got too tan over the summer, who said "nigga" but were adamant about not being Black and observed the differences in the ways we moved through the world. During a time of budding sexuality, crushes, and passing notes to boys in class, I felt largely invisible in that respect. I didn't necessarily want to be them or even to look like them. I wondered what I assumed was uncomplicated beauty must feel like.

For me, a dark-skinned girl, the concept of beauty seemed like something that would always and could only be complicated. On a personal level, on a systemic level, I observed that dark-skinned girls had to be exceptionally beautiful, luminous with perfectly unblemished skin, in order to be seen as desirable. And even then, that often still wasn't enough. These were all messages that I picked up without even knowing it, little unspoken truths about being Black and dark, particularly in America. Nevermind the wider, global context.

Several years ago, somewhere in my early twenties, I went out to lunch with one of my close friends, a young woman of Bengali descent. We were two writers, "women of color," trying to figure out our places in the very white and very male-dominated industry of film criticism, and so we had a kind of understanding. It was our first time really hanging out, just the two of us, and we ended up having one of those quiet, earnest, and intense conversations that people who feel like outsiders often have, the kind of conversation in which souls are bared.

At one point, our talk wound its way to comparing our South Asian and African backgrounds, specifically conceptions of beauty. I remember her sitting across from me at the small, cramped booth we shared, candidly recounting the pain of being the dark one in her family. She spoke of how she'd always felt ugly, inferior even, in comparison to her lighter female relatives. She spoke of how often, when she was a child, she had been encouraged by aunties to stay out of the sun, lest she get any darker.

As a dark-skinned woman from Ghana, a country where at the time Fair & Lovely bleaching cream billboards riddled the landscapes of big cities, I was empathetic to her pain. And I was struck, instantly, by the arbitrariness, the ridiculousness of this hierarchy of shade. From my perspective, her complexion seemed, by societal standards as I understood them at the time, desirable. Ideal. The idea of her as "dark" didn't register for me. I had grown up with Black, Asian, and Latinx girls who were her complexion and who were considered light skinned in contrast to me and, thus, more valuable.

Later I'd come to a wider understanding of the intricacies at play when we talk about skin color, when we hover nervously around words like "light skinned" and "dark skinned" before landing on the term "colorism," a term that sometimes seems to mean everything and nothing at once. It is commonly defined as prejudice or discrimination against individuals with a dark skin tone, usually operating within the same ethnic or racial group. This definition obscures what colorism really is at its core: straight up racism, a function and tool of white supremacy. In order to preserve whiteness, an arbitrary rubric was created to define Blackness, a rubric wholly uninterested in how Black people wish to define themselves. Looking back on that lunch, I think about how, even in conversation with a brown girl, I was still squeezing myself into this inconsistent hierarchy of color, clinging to this thing that was not of me in order to make sense of the world. I didn't have any of these realizations back then. Honestly, it wasn't until I began writing and thinking deeply about pop culture professionally that I truly began to contemplate all the ways in which we have been affected.

Loving and writing about pop culture means constantly having to ask questions, even when the questions don't necessarily have any tangible answers. This is the work that precedes moving a conversation forward. And as is the case with racism and sexism, and so many of the "isms" that seem to dominate and dictate the trajectories of our lives without our permission, questioning colorism and how it works isn't a straight path. The way these concepts operate in our daily lives is at once oppressive and ephemeral. Growing up a dark-skinned girl in America wasn't always this overwhelming cloud of oppression for me but rather a series of small moments, little storms, building up into a life.

Coming of age in the '90s and 2000s, I was acutely conscious of the fact that the Black cover girl on any given magazine, or the one Black love interest in any given movie, was going to be a light-skinned girl or brown-skinned girl. I knew that the dark-skinned mom or daughter on the sitcom would, midseason, miraculously transform into a light-skinned mom or daughter with no explanation, no chance to process or mourn.

One season, Aunt Viv on *The Fresh Prince of Bel-Air* was portrayed by the dark-skinned actress Janet Louise Hubert, who embodied the character with a kind of graceful wit and nonchalance so rarely seen in Black TV moms. In the next season, she'd been unceremoniously and without explanation replaced by a light-skinned actress, Daphne Maxwell Reid. Where Hubert had presence, Reid was just nice (a characterization which, itself, was a lazy "light-skin" trope).

I came to expect that the mom or the daughter or the friend or the love interest would never be dark, and if she was dark, she would never be framed as anything other than a one-liner generator. She would not be presented or seen by any of the other characters as desirable or powerful, and if she was, this would be a joke. I accepted all this as a given, never contemplating the *why* because part of my survival (and my conditioning) in this society meant seeing and knowing but never asking.

The existence of skin bleaching, hair straightening, and other forms of manipulation that some Black and brown women indulge in is often used in arguments about so-called cultural appropriation. When Black women wear blond weaves, aren't they appropriating "white culture"? Sometimes, a weave is just a weave, not the specter of self-hate. Sometimes, it's more complicated than that.

Lil' Kim has been steadily changing her appearance since at least 1999, beginning with blue contacts and platinum blond weaves before moving on to nose contouring, breast implants, nose jobs, and so on. She has talked, on several occasions, about her struggles with self-esteem. In a 1996 interview on *BET Talk*, just after the release of her first album, *Hard Core*, she opened up about the impact past relationships with men had on her: "When I was younger, I've had a lot of relationships where men used to tell me that I wasn't all that, that I was ugly and without them I would be nothing. Now that I'm older, I'm taking all of that and flipping it back on the men. I'm like look, I am somebody, I don't need you or any man 'cause I'm doing it myself. Now's the time to build up my self-esteem."

Later, in 2000, Kim told *Newsweek*: "All my life men have told me I wasn't pretty enough—even the men I was dating . . . It's always been men putting me down just like my dad. To this day when someone says I'm cute, I can't see it. I don't see it no matter what *anybody* says."

And like many, she has taken on the racism that surrounds her and subscribed to what we're all told is the "ideal" image of beauty: the fairest skin, the blondest hair. The difference between Kim and so many others who struggle with this specific kind of low self-esteem is that Kim has money and access to doctors willing to indulge and encourage her need to change herself into a different person. Add to this the pressure most women in entertainment feel to uphold unrealistic requirements of beauty. Perhaps the saddest thing about Kim's transformation is that it reflects a look that is very much celebrated and applauded—just not on her.

Azealia Banks was more blunt about why she chose to bleach her deep brown skin, using the infamous Whitenicious cream by Dencia, in a tweet from June 2016. "Depression," Banks wrote. "Watching lighter skinned women advance all while have worse music than mine is confusing." Later, in a Facebook Live video in July 2016, she said, "I don't really think it's important to discuss the cultural significance of skin bleaching anymore.

"Just as Black people in this world, you assimilate, and there are things you accept, not just out of necessity but things become norm because they just happen all the time," Banks added. She went on to explain that she sees and accepts skin bleaching as a form of "assimilation," a "continuation of the falsification of self with being a Black person in America." She then compared skin bleaching to wearing weaves or getting cosmetic surgery:

Nobody was upset when I was wearing 30-inch weaves and tearing out my edges and doing all that type of shit like that. You guys loved it, but what is the difference?

In a series of tweets from February 2015 (from her now suspended account), Banks also wrote: "The treatment I get for being a dark skinned woman just makes me want to lay down and die sometimes. They hate us, they treat us like dogs, then turn around and ask why we're mad. I don't care what anyone says: men in general despise dark skinned women."

If this is the conclusion a famous rapper comes to, what about the millions of nameless Black girls who lack the access that she has?

My own experience with my skin and my self-image and how I view beauty has always made me wary of the framing of the colorism issue at large. I've often felt trapped by the culture's preoccupation with beauty. The thought leader, artist, and educator Mandy Harris Williams often asks this question, which hit me like a wave the first time I saw her tweet it: "What is the beauty FOR, though?" Truly, what is it for? What do dark-skinned Black women actually gain with it and what do we lose without it?

Many articles and essays have been written about how Black women, and especially dark-skinned Black women, are considered the least desirable of all races. Headlines like "Why dark-skinned Black girls like me aren't getting married" highlight data that show that Black women are less likely to get responses from men on social media. Every three months, there is the same "light skint vs. dark skint" debate on Black Twitter, or some meme denigrating dark-skinned women once again makes the rounds, kicking up yet another conversation over whether heterosexual men find darker women attractive.

It's not that these realities aren't worthy of mention, or that they don't play a very real role in colorism. It's just that these discussions about dark women and their self-worth center far too heavily on people with frankly irrelevant opinions (namely men). How do we discuss the mechanics and harms of colorism without relying on these talking points?

When people talk about dark-skinned women in pop culture and society, the focus revolves around who does and does not desire dark women or whether we even desire ourselves. Is this useful? Perhaps it is, but I wonder how the constant framing of this issue hinders discussions about the other ways in which colorism affects us.

I am frustrated with the discussion about colorism, especially as a Black woman who writes and thinks about culture and images. After all, so much of how Black women begin to understand or conceptualize colorism in our own lives stems from our cultural iconography and imagery—how magazine cover girls and movie stars are almost exclusively light, with "Eurocentric" features.

If Beyoncé had a deeper complexion, would her dominance within the zeitgeist be as ubiquitous as it is? Would she be as revered? As desired? Would she be as beloved as she is by white and Black audiences alike? As her artistry has evolved, and become more political and more explicitly Black, she's gotten pushback and criticism from the white mainstream for her messages of Black empowerment. But how much more vitriolic would the responses be if she were darker? Would she even be able to explore those themes at all?

It would be disingenuous to say there have been *no* dark-skinned women who have broken barriers and found success in popular culture. Nina Simone, Cicely Tyson, Brenda Sykes, Lauryn Hill, Gabrielle Union, Judy Pace, Alek Wek, and Naomi Campbell are other names that illustrate this fact. Whoopi Goldberg became the first bankable Black female star in the '80s and '90s, carving out a niche for herself as a comedic, sometimes dramatic, actress that few dark-skinned, "unconventionally" attractive Black women had claimed before her.

Grace Jones is another icon in this respect, but an exotified icon, one whose dark skin has always been a marker of an othered and almost alienesque beauty. Of course, Jones herself was the chief architect of her androgynous persona, intentional and methodical with her presentation, a unique early example of a Black woman who crafted an image largely unlike anything that had been seen before. She was exciting. But what was exciting about her, sometimes, didn't translate smoothly enough in the mainstream.

I often think of the scene in *Boomerang* where Jones'

character, trying to seduce cocky ad exec Marcus (played by Eddie Murphy), asks, "You are going to turn down a pussy like this?" It's an iconic line, but it's played for laughs in a very specific way, juxtaposed against the lighter-skinned, softer, more acceptable love interest Halle Berry.

Today, there is a slightly wider array of visible dark-skinned women in mainstream pop culture, from up-and-coming singer Normani to *Orange Is the New Black* actress Danielle Brooks. But the super A-listers, the Lupitas and Violas of the pop cultural landscape, are a relatively new phenomenon. Only ten years ago, for instance, the idea of a blockbuster horror film like *Us*, about a dark-skinned family of four, with a dark-skinned actress in the lead role, would not feel realistic.

Something we all know: the biggest Black female stars have always been lighter skinned. Lena Horne, Dorothy Dandridge, Halle Berry, Beyoncé, Rihanna, and others have made it to the upper echelons of Hollywood partly because of their hard work and talent (I will never take that away from them) and partly because having lighter skin, wavy 3C hair, and Eurocentric features has been a key advantage to making it in a pop cultural landscape that loves the things Black women produce but doesn't love Black women in all their forms.

This does not negate the fact that these women, regardless of their complexions, have faced obstacles and barriers on the way to that success because of their race. (Lena Horne, for instance, lost out on a deeply sought-after and deserved role of a Black woman passing as white in 1951's *Showboat* to white actress Ava Gardner because Hollywood execs couldn't abide the idea of Horne kissing her white male love interest on screen.) But the truth still stands: light-skinned Black women have always been deemed more beautiful and therefore more palatable, more marketable, for mainstream audiences.

This is a reality of the industry that has not totally gone away, even in the wake of more dark-skinned stars experiencing success. When studio executives commissioned an X-Men franchise reboot in 2016, instead of replacing Halle Berry, who played Storm in several films in the franchise, with a dark-skinned actress (more accurate to the portrayal of Ororo "Storm" Munroe in the comics), they chose light-skinned actress Alexandra Shipp.

Shipp received backlash for the casting. Later, she waxed poetic about a Storm movie starring herself, Halle Berry, Amandla Stenberg, and Yara Shahidi, all playing Storm at different stages of the character's life (which is odd, as Stenberg and Shahidi are not that far in age from Shipp herself). Her hypothetical vision was emblematic of a very real problem in Hollywood—the fact that the same pool of teen to twenty-something-year-old Black actresses keeps coming up, and they're all light. There's this assumption with representation that we must always celebrate the wins of people with whom we share some facet of identity as our own, without critiquing the ways in which their privilege allows them to navigate the world. There's an idea that the only value in representation is affirmation when, actually, its value is varied and complicated. Colorism is one of these complications.

In June 2018, Rebecca Theodore-Vachon, a prominent Black female film critic, posited a simple question on Twitter. "We have a problem," she wrote. "Can anyone name 3 darker-skinned A-List Black actresses UNDER the age of 30 and currently getting offered lead roles? Because I can easily list at least 5–6 lighter skinned/mixed race who are."

My first reaction to this tweet was, "Yikes." I knew, even as the conversation developed and the thread lengthened and Black women across Twitter racked their brains to come up with a robust list of dark-skinned A-list Black women under the age of thirty, they wouldn't.

An hour went by after Rebecca's initial tweet and no one had managed to come up with any names. Eventually, Letitia Wright, the then-twenty-four-year-old actress who had starred in a gripping episode of *Black Mirror* and had just made her major film debut in *Black Panther* as Shuri, was offered up. (At the time, Marsai Martin's *Little* had yet to debut—she, fourteen at the time, would have *maybe* been a plausible addition to the list, as would then-twenty-six-year-old *If Beale Street Could Talk* star Kiki Layne.)

Some people suggested that it was hard to consider Letitia "A-list" so early in her career, despite an impressive start. Over thirty was easier—there was Lupita, of course, and Angela Bassett, and Gabrielle Union, Issa Rae, and Viola Davis. But eventually, the conversation petered out with Rebecca's original point made: despite the strides that have been made, Hollywood still has a colorism problem.

Those dark-skinned Black actresses who are A-list in their thirties and beyond—we forget how long it took them to get there. Whoopi Goldberg, the first bankable, dark-skinned Black actress in Hollywood who experienced her peak during the '80s and '90s, made her big splash with the much-lauded *The Color Purple*. She was thirty when the film came out, and though she would work steadily in between with other hits like *Jumpin' Jack Flash*, she was thirty-five when her megahit, *Ghost*, came out in 1990.

Unlike white actresses, such as Gwyneth Paltrow and Kate Winslet and Jennifer Lawrence, or light actresses like Halle Berry, Zendaya, Yara Shahidi, and Amandla Stenberg, these dark-skinned Black actresses did not build their careers in the spotlight, constantly feted and admired as they worked on their craft. No, they hustled for years to get the recognition that their white and lighter-skinned counterparts captured early on.

Jennifer Lawrence was twenty-one when she won her first Oscar and by twenty-two was the star of two major blockbuster franchises. Compare this to Issa Rae, who had to build her own platform via YouTube in her twenties to finally get her own HBO show on the air when she turned thirty. Or Lupita Nyong'o, who was thirty years old when she appeared in her first movie, a supporting role in 2013's *12 Years A Slave*. It would take another six years for Nyong'o, at age thirty-six, to get her first actual lead starring role, in Jordan Peele's *Us*.

Viola Davis was starring in bit parts on *Law & Order* ten years before she was first nominated for an Oscar in

2009. She sees the incongruity, the realities of what being a woman who looks like her has wrought in her career and in her life. At the Women in the World L.A. Salon in 2018, Davis said, "I got the Oscar. I got the Emmy. I've got two Tonys. I've done Broadway. I've done off-Broadway. I've done TV. I've done film. I've done all of it."

She continued:

"I have a career that's probably comparable to Meryl Streep, Julianne Moore, Sigourney Weaver. They all came out of Yale. They came out of Juilliard. They came out of NYU. They had the same path as me, and yet, I am nowhere near them. Not as far as money, not as far as job opportunities—nowhere close to it. But I have to get on that phone and people say, 'You're a Black Meryl Streep. There is no one like you.' Okay, then if there's no one like me, you think I'm that, you pay me what I'm worth. You give me what I'm worth."

The use of the word "worth" in relation to an older, dark-skinned Black actress in the Hollywood capitalist machine is tenuous, and telling. Worth, after all, is what racism and colorism revolves around, what they always boil down to.

When *Vanity Fair* chose Davis to be its July/August 2020 cover girl, the cover was lauded as being the first in the magazine's thirty-seven-year history to be shot by a black photographer, Dario Calmese. In the image, Davis has a large curly afro, and sits wearing a sculptural midnight-blue backless gown, her back to us, her face in profile, a hand resting on her hip. Her exposed back, the skin dark and silky and smooth, is the focal point. A quote, from her, "My entire life has been a protest," is written in bold white letters against the blue background.

A week before the magazine hit the stands, Calmese did an interview with the *New York Times* in which he revealed that when he got the job, he "did not know that this was a moment to say something."

But, "I knew this was a moment to be, like, extra black."

The image, on its own, has a kind of regal elegance, yes. It invites us to consider not only Davis' beauty but her power. But it is also in specific reference to another, more famous image—an 1863 portrait of an enslaved man with a scarred, mutilated back called "The Scourged Back." Calmese had decided just days before the shoot to re-create the photo with Davis as subject.

"When you look at it [The Scourged Back], it is gruesome and harsh," he said. But Calmese also saw in it elements that could inform his upcoming portrait: "He pushes back more toward the camera. His hand is at his waist—you know that line, with his profile going down the arm and coming back. And so I was like: I can re-create this."

You can re-create this, yes. But why?

The cover image itself is fine, though it is a lazy conflation to make. I'm interested in what makes an artistic mind draw such strong parallels between *that* particular photo of *that* particular enslaved man and Davis. Why was a history of violence and abuse grafted onto this image, onto her body, and would that be the case if she were a lighter-skinned woman? Obviously, no. Because it is dark women who so often have to hold and represent the pain and trauma of Black memory, even in moments when they are ostensibly being celebrated for things that have nothing to do with pain and trauma.

Too much is projected onto Black women with dark skin that has nothing to do with them, with their lived experiences, with their potential to break free of being condensed down to what their skin means to everyone but themselves.

This isn't just an issue when it comes to who gets access to fame or money or prestige, though. It manifests itself in other ways within Black culture and between Black people. It manifests in the tendency for dark-skinned Black women to take on the brunt of emotional labor in friendships without reciprocity. It manifests in dark-skinned women being overlooked by potential Black romantic and sexual partners. It manifests itself from the day you are born.

A video went briefly viral across YouTube and Twitter in the spring of 2019. It features a mother, Biannca Prince, a biracial Instagram baddie with over a million followers, in the aftermath of giving birth to a healthy baby daughter. As a nurse coddles the infant, Biannca, skin the shade of coffee with heavy cream, lies silent in a hospital bed. She looks despondent, maybe even a little disinterested. "I thought she would have pretty eyes," she says, when she realizes her daughter's eyes are brown, not blue. "If you look at her nail beds, her ears. They're dark. She's going to be dark."

"But she's beautiful," a nurse chimes in. Biannca does not respond.

A more careful look suggests that Biannca isn't simply disinterested—she's devastated. At one point, the father, a dark-skinned Black man who is filming the video for their popular YouTube channel, says "sorry" when she once again laments the baby's dark brown eyes.

Herein lies the illogical and deeply painful nature of colorism: an infant, not even an hour old, already being appraised over how light or how dark she is. Her value being assessed by her own mother, who by saying "I thought she would have pretty eyes" is establishing even in these precious early moments that her daughter's eyes aren't pretty—her ears aren't pretty, her hands aren't pretty—*she* is not pretty and, therefore, in a world that requires/ only values women for their looks, not valuable.

It's strange, almost funny (if it weren't so sad) that a young biracial Black woman can see the beauty in a dark-skinned Black man, see it enough to fuck him, marry him, build a life with him, but can't see that beauty in her own daughter. There's something twisted in that, isn't there? In loving a dark Black man but not wanting to see any trace of him in the children you bear?

Features, hair texture, "phenotype" are just as much a part of this conversation as skin tone is. All these facets, these requirements for beauty, result in a culture where darker-skinned women often have to exhibit certain characteristics outside of color in order to access power, safety, love. Beauty is a powerful cultural currency, especially for women, who are expected to be beautiful until the day they die and taught that no matter how smart or talented they are their beauty (or lack thereof) is key.

Consider this tweet, posted by a Black man in January 2019: "Ari Lennox and Teyana Taylor's ability to have dangerously high sex appeal while simultaneously looking like rottweilers will always amaze me."

Ari Lennox and Teyana Taylor, soul and R&B singers, have very different vibes. Ari is a soul singer, a self-professed "Shea Butter Baby" who rocks her hair in natural springy curls and looks like she smells good. Teyana is a dancer, slightly androgynous, popular on social media as much for her slick hip-hop–infused R&B as she is for her resplendently ripped abs. Both women are objectively beautiful. Both women have wide noses, thick lips, very *Black* features.

Not long after the tweet was sent, it generated yet another debate about colorism and the disrespect of visibly Black women in the public eye. Many people called the tweet out, but a surprisingly large number of the almost 3,000 commenters on the thread also laughed along and agreed. This time, though, Ari Lennox weighed in. Lennox, then twenty-nine, tweeted (and later deleted): "People hate Blackness so bad." In an Instagram Live stream posted not long after, tears in her eyes, she added: "I'm not fucking with that shit. How people hate Black people so much, how Black people can sit up here and say, 'That's not my problem.' Or, 'She does look like a rott- weiler.' And you want to talk about, 'Oh, people are so sensitive, they want us to cancel freedom of speech.' *Why is this your speech*?" The colorism conversation always ends with a question, not an answer. The first time I saw this, the tears in Lennox's eyes, the indignation in her voice, I latched on to that question. *Why is this your speech?* Activ- ist Michaela Angela Davis, a light-skinned Black woman herself, has advocated for recognizing privileges and bi- ases, and simply talking it out. "Acting like it doesn't exist doesn't heal . . . America as a family," Davis said during Soledad O'Brien's CNN special *Who Is Black in Amer- ica?* in 2012. "This is our taboo issue that brings up so much. It triggers a lot of Black girl pain. It triggers a lot of secrets. It triggers a lot of bias. It triggers a lot of emo- tional things. And like any family, when we go into our history and say this horrible thing created this character- istic, people don't want to look at it. But this is the road to healing, right? This is the only way we're going to feel whole: is we talk about where we're fractured."

But how do you talk about something when people do not want to acknowledge it exists? That denial, after all, is how colorism creeps into the culture we consume with ruthless efficiency. There's a cunning to colorism, an in- sidious ability for it to spring up even in situations with the best intentions. Take, for instance, the HBO series *Lovecraft Country,* a sci-fi horror anthology that follows the adventures and trials of a Black family in 1950s Chicago.

The lead actress on the show was light-skinned, biracial actress Jurnee Smollett, who played Letitia "Leti" Lewis. Wunmi Mosaku played Ruby, her sister, the physical antithesis of Leti. Where Leti is small, rail thin, and light, Ruby is a strikingly beautiful, tall, dark-skinned, fat Black woman.

At first, this contrast feels too intentional to go unexplored, especially given the ongoing tension between the sisters throughout the ten-episode first season. Much of Ruby's story arc, after all, revolves around her magically embodying the form of a thin white woman in order to more freely navigate the world. But these realities of how Leti and Ruby experience the world are never really discussed with intention or care.

In an interview with writer Brooke Obie for Shondaland in 2020, *Lovecraft Country* showrunner Misha Green (herself a light brown–skinned woman) was asked how the history of colorism within Black communities informed the creation of the characters and their storylines.

"It didn't," said Green. "We had a lot of conversations about colorism in the room, but I didn't want to specifically whittle down the stories to colorism, honestly. We talked about it a lot in the room, because obviously it's so pervasive in our culture right now that it's hard not to talk about it, but I wanted to say everything is not about colorism. So therefore I don't want to just turn this story of these sisters, or of these characters, [into] colorism."

The decision to avoid colorism altogether so as not

to "whittle down" the story of these characters, a story that does so much to explore the realities and the terrors of being Black in a world that hates Blackness, is an interesting one. To be aware that colorism exists and do nothing to actively counter it is also an interesting choice. You become the problem you say you want to solve.

And indeed, throughout the series, while Ruby (played flawlessly by Mosaku) has moments that genuinely transcend the most common tropes we see in depictions of dark-skinned, fat Black women, this is undercut by all the ways in which the show actively perpetuates these tropes. For instance, in all the discourse that the show generated when it initially aired, so much of the debate around Ruby clung to the idea that she was somehow duplicitous, "mean," angry, and jealous of her sister—ignoring the fact that she had genuine, valid reasons to be distrustful of her.

This implicit, subconscious elevation of lighter-skinned women is rampant in the culture.

It's wildly harmful to deny that colorism benefits lighter-skinned people, even though they experience racism. It's harmful not to recognize that, to dismiss and deny. Space must be made. There are things we must admit if we are to get past colorism. For one thing, we must admit that a certain privilege, however hard to pin down, does exist for lighter people. We must admit that colorism, as a whole, has layers, is as complicated as it is destructive. We must acknowledge and make space for the fact that, when it comes to dark-skinned Black women and beauty, not every Black woman can subvert the beauty standards that oppress her—or even necessarily wants to. Skin bleaching, weaves, and their ilk are as much modes of survival and assimilation as they are anything else. But ultimately, and most importantly, in talking about where we're fractured, we must also talk about how we're whole.

Sometimes, I think, just saying the thing/acknowledging the realities of all this goes a long way. So much of healing, both personal and communal, starts first with acceptance and acknowledgment of the wound, not once, but constantly. The light-skinned Stenberg, whose casting in the film *The Hate U Give* sparked criticism because the character in the book on which it is based had been specifically described as dark, shared the following on Instagram in July 2020:

> It's a disservice to the fight for liberation and the deconstruction of white supremacy to distance yourself from your whiteness. I say that as someone who in the past has dissociated myself from my own whiteness for fear of not being seen as Black by my Black community. However, I understand now how counterproductive and obtuse it is to refuse to recognize the ways in which you benefit from proximity to whiteness. Whether that's the color of your skin and the ways in which you benefit from colorism. Or the way you were so-

cialized and the social languages you were taught to speak that grant you access to white approval. White supremacy is a complex and insidious lattice of oppression and that means that the way we experience privilege works in degrees. And it's our job to constantly clock those mechanisms at work and work against them.

Gestures like these are not just gestures, they are everything. Light-skinned Black women and femmes who publicly accept the role they play in a messed-up system, who acknowledge that they must do better rather than deflect their own complicity, are tangentially forcing everyone else to do so. This includes the casting directors and screenwriters and filmmakers who seek "types" that they believe are more palatable. This is a kind of starting point, a place from which to grow.

But the dark girl will not become whole from gestures of solidarity alone, from talking about the fractures that she herself did not create. The idea of wholeness, of not compartmentalizing my hang-ups about the way that I look, what *kind* of a Black girl I am, has been key to my healing. To become free, I've had to reject these things while also accepting they exist. Interrogating my speech, interrogating the narrative I create around my own beauty, has unlocked an understanding for me about being a Black girl, a dark girl. The understanding is: I see very clearly the mechanisms at play, designed to disenfranchise, oppress, deny me access. I see them clearly, but I do not accept them as an inevitability, the way I accepted that Aunt Viv would be dark skinned one day and light skinned the next.

Mae Jemison

Mae Jemison: On September 12, 1992, launch day of the STS-47 Spacelab-J mission on space shuttle *Endeavour*, NASA astronaut Mae Jemison waits as her suit technician, Sharon McDougle, performs an unpressurized and pressurized leak check on her spacesuit at the Operations and Checkout Building at Kennedy Space Center. Image Credit: NASA.

#CardiBIsSoProblematic

In October 2018, Cardi B went on an Instagram tirade. She uploaded one, two, three, eventually nine
videos in which she went off on her apparent neme-
sis, Nicki Minaj. Nicki had allegedly told lies about her,
and Cardi wanted to set the record straight. In each uploaded clip, she disputed Nicki's recent claims on an episode of her show *Queen Radio* that Cardi was "ragged" by
Nicki's associate (friend seems too strong a word) Rah
Ali during their infamous altercation at a *Harper's BA-
ZAAR* party that past September.

You may remember this incident, or at the very least
the dramatic paparazzi photos of its aftermath: Cardi

dressed in an opulent lacy red Dolce and Gabbana gown, barefoot (she had thrown her stiletto at Minaj earlier), being escorted out of the party flanked by security guards. On her face, carefully fixed like a mask, an expression of concentrated unbotheredness. And if you looked closely, there, just above her left eyebrow: a large, round, raised red knot on her forehead. (A year later, Cardi would re-create this photo in a cover spread for *Harper's BAZAAR*, complete with red evening gown, bare feet, and a Cinderella-esque forgotten stiletto shoe spotlit in the background.)

According to Cardi, the fight was really the inevitable result of what she felt had been a long-simmering whisper campaign against her, orchestrated by Nicki. In her Instagram polemic, she alleged that Nicki had actively tried to stop her bag on several occasions, had allowed and even encouraged her fanbase to harass Cardi, had perpetuated the idea that Cardi was disrespectful and ungrateful to the self-professed Queen of Rap, and, perhaps worst of all, had questioned Cardi's parenting of her newborn baby girl, Kulture.

The rant in its entirety was peak Cardi: at the height of her career, young, reckless, outspoken, and unapologetic. Without a second thought of the potential consequences, she was coming for Nicki Minaj, a powerful and beloved hip-hop colossus with a fiercely passionate and devoted contingent of fans and stans.

At times, it has been Cardi's seeming disregard for the consequences of what she says that has attracted me to her music, and to her as a pop cultural figure overall. And yet it has been this very same disregard that has also at times repelled me and, ultimately, forced me to grapple with the unspoken truths of her celebrity, of celebrity in general, in more meaningful and exacting ways.

The exciting thing about Cardi is also the exhausting thing about Cardi: she's always a topic of discussion on the gossip sites and on Black Twitter. She's invariably doing or saying something that gets people talking. At any one moment, she's breaking some industry record for women in music, or she's a judge on a reality show about hip-hop questioning if a female contestant is sexy and marketable enough to make it, or she's twerking while eight months pregnant on the main stage at Coachella, or she's showing up to court to face assault charges in a ridiculous and amazing floor-length feathered coat, or she's interviewing Bernie Sanders about healthcare for all and declaring "HEALTH OVER CAPITALISM," or she's in a rage spiral on Instagram Live, saying something like, "Access Hollywood, suck my whole dick. Suck a dick, I hope your fucking mom catch AIDS bitch. The fuck?! Y'all niggas is crazy. Y'all niggas is crazy!" Millions of people are watching her every move.

Following the career trajectory of Belcalis "Cardi B" Almanzar, even casually, is sometimes like riding a janky Top Spin at an amusement park, a constant back-and-forth between one dizzying headline and the next, a continual lurch from one realization about what she represents (or doesn't represent) to another. I've danced joyfully to her music; her first two mixtapes may not have reinvented the wheel, but they are fun, and her first album, *Invasion of Privacy*, is in my estimation a genuinely great debut. I've rooted for her. I've been disappointed in her. I've struggled with her. I've even questioned the merits of including an essay about her in this book at all. There's the constant debate around her Blackness, for one thing, and her history of making wildly transphobic and colorist statements, for another.

Recently, I was discussing my apprehension with a friend who said, "Girl, it's just Cardi B. She's just a rapper. It's really not that deep." Cardi, like so many Black women in pop culture, is not taken seriously—as an artist, as a celebrity, as a political thinker (yes), as a person. And there's a danger in not taking her and other contemporary Black women rappers—Nicki Minaj, Megan Thee Stallion, Flo Milli, Saweetie—seriously, because they tell us so much about the culture and about ourselves. Statements like "it's really not that deep" belie the fact that, on some level, it really is.

Cardi is just a rapper, sure, and depending on whom you talk to, not an especially talented one at that. And yet, there's so much to mine from her music and her success, so much concerning the positioning of certain Black women in pop culture, particularly hip-hop. In Cardi, we can consider the fallacies and frailties of celebrity, wealth, representation, and how these things aren't necessarily the things that will get us free—Black women, or anyone else for that matter.

The allure of Cardi B has always been that she's both an underdog and an aspirational model. In less than a decade, Cardi went from a popular stripper to a prolific Instagram personality to a comedienne to a reality TV star to a mixtape diva to one of the highest-selling female rappers of all time. When she first came on the scene, certain circles (particularly white, liberal circles) championed her as a kind of feminist hero.

The narrative for Cardi, one that was ultimately thrust upon her by some of these circles, was that she made it out the hood and out the strip club and thus, by virtue of doing that and that alone, experienced the greatest achievement of her life. This narrative, while on the surface celebratory, is also revelatory about how sex work is often viewed, even by those who say they champion sex workers: it is not so much a choice as a kind of moral failing or, if the person standing in judgment is feeling generous, an affliction, a joyless option, something that happens *to* you on the road to survival. There's this tendency for people to frame sex work as either inherently empowering, a radical act, or inherently demeaning, something to be saved from. This obscures the fact that sex work is labor and that sex workers are only revolutionary if they so choose.

To hear her tell it, at nineteen years old Cardi chose her path consciously. Kicked out of her mother's home as a teenager and later in an abusive relationship, Cardi found in stripping a means of personal and financial autonomy. As a public figure, Cardi pushes up against narratives that declare that this is never the case for sex work. She shares videos on her Instagram wearing her stripping clothes backstage or twerking at the club, matter-of-factly. Yes, she is always angling for the next side hustle, but she never acts like what she was doing was anything other than her choice and, most importantly, a job that she was incredibly good at. As her early online popularity grew, she posted videos that showcased her unique mix of sexuality and humor, like the viral clip of her walking down some random hotel hallway clad in a hip-hugging pencil skirt and a sparkly bra. "It's cold outside," she says, laughing, "But a ho never gets cold!"

Cardi has a knack for this—deflecting with humor the politics of shame and respectability that constantly come her way. Humor, after all, has always been an effective tool for disarming those who would want to humiliate you. In this way, Cardi has an innate ability to lean fully into the things that she's supposed to want to move away from. This is one of her greatest talents.

I remember people were horrified when, at age twenty-five, at the height of her "Bodak Yellow" popularity and on the cusp of the release of her first album, Cardi decided to have a child, Kulture, with then-fiancé and current on-again-off-again husband, Offset. On social media and in the comments of gossip sites like The Shade Room, people were vocal in their confusion. She was at her peak, and now she was having a *baby*? In the middle of an album rollout? With *that* dude? Wasn't this the kiss of death to a career that had barely begun? Then there was the debacle surrounding her subsequent brief split from Offset: ashy dudes came out of the woodwork on social media demanding that she take him back, despite his numerous (documented) instances of cheating on her. When she did in fact reconcile with him, she was criticized by fans and haters alike (if there is a difference) for being a "bird."

Cardi constantly undermines and complicates people's illusions about her. Her entry into the industry conjured up a compelling version of the ultimate American fantasy. Anyone in America can make it on one's own terms, her come up told us; anyone can find fame and fortune without losing oneself. And now the reality of a child and a messy, complicated relationship with a cheating spouse intruded on that illusion. Fans wanted Cardi to be authentic, sure, but not to be herself. They wanted her to be authentic to the fantasy. The fantasy isn't supposed to include mistakes. It isn't supposed to include messiness.

Cardi is loud. She's ratchet. Her style, from her two-inch-long nails by nail tech Jenny Bui in the Bronx to her ever-changing array of colorful wigs, is in keeping with a tradition of Black women rappers who use ostentation and sexuality as scaffolding for their personas. But there's a joyful irreverence to her persona that adds to her appeal, a seemingly unfiltered, unpracticed way of existing in a landscape that in the past has constantly asked Black women to exist, yes, but on very specific terms. This is a tightrope so many Black women in the mainstream have to walk to be their authentic selves—

without becoming caricatures. For Cardi, walking that tightrope has been easier because of the way she looks.

Cardi obviously isn't the first female rapper. She's certainly not the first Black woman in mainstream culture who has been ratchet, loud, hood. Black women rappers who came before her include Sister Souljah, Trina, Lil' Kim, Missy Elliott, and Foxy Brown. But in twenty years, there's never been a dark-skinned female rapper, outside of Foxy Brown or Lauryn Hill, who has made it this far. (Azealia Banks came close. But not anything like Cardi.)

We have to consider, after all, what the rap game, particularly for women, looked like five, ten, twenty years before Nicki or Cardi came along. There was a Golden Age in female hip-hop when several female emcees were out there and were thriving. Lil' Kim and Foxy, Missy and Lauryn, Rah Digga and Remy Ma, and a slew of other rappers between the late '90s and mid-2000s released hit singles, even collaborated together.

That abundance died out as some female rappers retired, pursued other avenues (Queen Latifah, for instance, built an A-list Hollywood career and a beauty empire), or, in Lil' Kim's and Remy Ma's cases, were absent thanks to prison bids. And then, there was a drought of talent for many years. There were several Black female rappers during this in-between time, but no one who broke through until Nicki Minaj quenched the culture's thirst for a badass, sexy female rapper who actually had bars. For ten years, Nicki dominated the mainstream, making a name for herself through her features on other rappers' tracks.

We had Nicki, the rightful Queen, and then a smattering of women rappers with popular online or underground followings, all orbiting Nicki, staying out of her way but thriving in their own lanes. And then came Cardi. With Cardi, for the first time in probably twenty years, we had more than one Black woman breaking records and pulling in hype. And also, a woman ready and willing to confront the idea that there can be only one dominant woman rapper in the game.

The nine videos Cardi posted to Instagram in October 2018 calling out Nicki and stating that she was down to fight, to talk, "it's whatever," were the culmination of a beef that is long and sordid, and possibly one that goes back further than we know. The first public shots were fired in 2017. Cardi came out onstage to support Remy Ma during a concert, after Ma had, just weeks earlier, released the scathing diss track targeted at Nicki, "Shether." Then in May, Nicki seemed to take aim at Cardi in a Katy Perry song called "Swish Swish."

"Silly rap beefs just get me more checks/My life is a movie, I'm never off set/Me and my amigos (no, not Offset)," Nicki rapped. The Offset line seemed like a clear allusion to Cardi. By alluding to Cardi's husband, Nicki was making her stance clear—this beef with Cardi was largely irrelevant to her, simply free publicity. Not long after "Swish Swish" was released, Cardi took to Instagram to talk about how much she hated sneak dissing.

"A bitch like me," she said, "I was happier when I was macking in the hood. This shit right here is so fake. When I used to be a regular bitch from the Bronx—a hood bitch—when somebody used to be fake to me, it was cool because I could approach a bitch and punch her right in her closure . . . Now that I'm in the industry, you don't work like that. Just have to watch shit go, watch shit go."

For a while, things were calm, the two were maybe even on good terms. There was a moment in July 2017 when Nicki was seen bopping to "Bodak Yellow" at the club. In August of the same year Cardi tried to clear up feud rumors in an interview with *Billboard* magazine. "I don't really want problems with anybody. I don't want to be, like, queen . . . I just wanna make music and make money. I really don't have time to look at other women, what they doing. I'm myself, you know what I'm saying? Nobody got a problem with me. I don't got a problem with them. If somebody got a problem I don't really got to do that whole industry beef. I get it poppin' with these hands."

In September 2017, when "Bodak Yellow" hit number one, making Cardi the first female rapper since Lauryn Hill to reach that record, Nicki tweeted: "Congratulations to a fellow New Yawka on a Record Breaking achievement. Bardi, this is the only thing that matters! Enjoy it."

But whatever goodwill the two had built up melted away with "MotorSport," the single from the Migos album *Culture II*. We may never really know what happened, but early on there were stories that Nicki wasn't happy that Cardi would be included on the song, that Cardi wasn't happy with Nicki's original verse, that at the last minute, Nicki came in with a whole new verse that supposedly "sonned" Cardi. This, apparently, was the final straw, and their internet mentions were then strewn with petty subliminal likes and cryptic, passive-aggressive callouts. Then there was the altercation at *Harper's BAZAAR* and eventually rants from Nicki about Cardi on Minaj's *Queen Radio* show.

The beef between Cardi and Nicki, the squashing of the beef, the debate about the beef, all of it may have been fun to watch play out on a deeply petty level, but none of it is as significant as this: two Black women, both young, both sexy, both producing catchy and accessible music, existing in the same space at the same time, a space that society for so long has deluded them (and all of us) into believing only has room for one. Their success and the shots they take at one another suggest, on some level, that they have bought into this delusion.

Power, especially the dark kind of power—power that thrives in systems like capitalism and white supremacy and hetero-patriarchy—breaks the world down into hierarchies that don't exist. Nicki and Cardi's beef is emblematic of this manufactured hustle for dominance, and the casualties of it.

The beef with Nicki was, to my mind, one of the first times Cardi came into real conflict as not just an internet star but a major player in the rap game. The beef brought much to the fore, including the overwhelming contrast between Nicki, now over ten years in the game of navigating her own celebrity, and Cardi, new to fame and steeped in the culture of social media. On her *Queen Radio* show shortly after the *Harper's BAZAAR* incident, Nicki discussed how embarrassed she was by the almost-fight between her and Cardi; how she felt "mortified" by the fact that this was taking place among the "upper-echelon" of the fashion industry. She made clear that even she must navigate within the lines of respectability, and Cardi, so quick to pop off, must now do the same. I wonder if Nicki sees herself in Cardi at all.

In some sense, Cardi opened the floodgates. Since her come up, women rappers, including Megan Thee Stallion, Saweetie, and Doja Cat, have emerged onto the scene and garnered the same kind of record-breaking numbers and *Billboard* 100 hits that initially made Cardi feel like such an anomaly.

Cardi's Blackness isn't an anomaly, but it has often been treated as such. She is absolutely everything that white America copies and then calls "ghetto" or "ratchet" when Black women rock it. Her hoodness is authentic to her experience and, along with her Blackness, is what made her famous, the antithesis of so many Black stars of yesteryear, from Lena Horne to Whitney Houston, who had to mold themselves into a more palatable version of Blackness in order to make it.

Women like Cardi, after all, aren't supposed to make

it, and if they make it that is because they have molded themselves into something approaching authenticity, but not quite authentic to themselves. When I think about Cardi, I think a lot about this idea of "authenticity" and what it means to be authentic once you've crossed over into the mainstream. At what point does authenticity become performance, and vice versa? Can you ever reconcile the two? I'm of two minds, constantly, about this. But for Cardi, it's a question that she is constantly navigating with her fame.

In late 2018, Cardi touched down at a Perth, Australia, airport where paparazzi and fans were waiting for her. When she declined to take pictures with the group, one of them, an older white woman, shouted, "That's why your husband left you!" This was at the height of the Cardi/Offset drama, after a video of him allegedly having sex with another woman was leaked online. Cardi's publicist was caught on camera yelling at the woman, who instantly began to play the victim. She cowered and said the publicist's behavior was "uncalled for." The incident was representative of Cardi's entire situation as a Black woman in the public eye, a Black woman in the white mainstream, expected to be "on" at all times, particularly for white onlookers. Comments under Cardi's Instagram posts about the incident were full of mostly brown and Black fans chiding her for having a "ghetto" publicist, for lacking decorum in her newfound fame.

Cardi's response to this criticism in a video post was,

I think, the perfect distillation of her struggle to remain herself even as her star (and the pressures of stardom) rises. She said:

> Stop telling me how I need to act like another celebrity. "This person would never. You need to handle your situation like this celebrity . . ." That's not me. That's not me. Sometimes, I don't even feel like I'm a celebrity because the standards and the way you expect these celebrities to act, hoe, that is *not me* motherfucker. I don't talk like that, I don't act like that. I'm just doing my motherfucking job. I'm just getting my coins. I'mma handle this shit how I handle it. I've been acting like this, I've been this way my whole entire life. So stop it. Your favorite celebrities be telling me, "I wish I could express myself the way you express yourself. I'm so happy that you're fucking speaking up for us." So I don't give a fuck.

The fact that Cardi navigated this situation successfully in real time, with no filter, is remarkable. The fact that she exists, however messily, is a small medallion of hope for girls like her. But representation is a trap, one I constantly fall into myself. I know some Black women don't consider Cardi Black. I know that she's said and done things in the past that are straight up unacceptable, period. I understand that for me there's a kind of privilege in being able to "grapple" with these things.

Cardi is an Afro-Latina, she's Caribbean, she's biracial, she's half Dominican, half Trinidadian. Many of these things—the fact that she speaks Spanish, for instance—make some Black people see her as not Black, but as something adjacent to Blackness, and therefore fair game for debate: is she Black, and if she isn't, does she have a right to take up space within hip-hop?

Amid the Cardi/Nicki beef in the fall of 2018, Nicki, on her *Queen Radio* show, accused Cardi of once calling Black women "roaches." (Cardi's defense against this critique is that she calls everyone roaches, including herself, which says far more about her and her relationship to Blackness than perhaps she may realize.) Stating that Cardi "came into my culture" (Nicki meant hip-hop culture, but this could easily be construed as Black culture) uninvited, Nicki said, "Oh, 'cause she's not Black. Cause we got receipts for that too." I found this interesting when I heard it, wondering what the receipts were, given the fact that, like Cardi, Nicki is Trinidadian (and often raps about her "mixed" looks).

For her part, Cardi says she identifies as a Black woman—she often makes this assertion specifically in moments when her Blackness is questioned or challenged, or when she's called out for colorist and anti-Black behavior. In a 2018 interview with Zendaya for *CR Fashion Book*, Cardi expressed frustration surrounding the debate about whether she's Black, and/or whether she identifies as Black.

"One thing that always bothers me is that people

know so little about my culture. We are Caribbean people. And a lot of people be attacking me because they
feel like I don't be saying that I'm Black," she said.

"Some people want to decide if you're Black or not, depending on your skin complexion, because they don't understand Caribbean people or our culture . . . I don't got
to tell you that I'm Black. I expect you to know it."

In June 2019, on Instagram Live, Cardi again talked
about her frustration with being mistaken for Mexican
and/or non-Black because she can speak Spanish. "I'm
not Mexican at all. I'm West Indian and I'm Dominican.
I speak Spanish because I'm Dominican. And it's like, 'So
what's the difference between Dominican and Mexican?'
And it's like, everything! People just don't be understanding shit. It's like, 'Cardi's Latin, she's not Black.' And it's
like, 'Bro, my features don't come from . . . white people
fucking, OK?' And they always wanna race-bait when it
comes to me . . . I have Afro features. 'Oh, but your parents
are light-skinned'—alright, but my grandparents aren't."

She then seemingly alluded, once again, to Nicki
Minaj—"It's crazy because some island women, some
artists that are from the same islands as me, people will
be like, 'Oh they're Black.' But because Cardi speaks
Spanish to people, she's not Black, even though we have
similar features, same skin complexion. But no, they want
to not put Cardi in it because I speak Spanish."

The debate about Cardi's Blackness, I've come to realize, is implicitly about something else. Her beefs, her
transgressions, her success . . . it all comes down to the

currency and capital of color. Color is powerful, and power. It is difficult, nuanced, unwieldy. It's not enough to lay the laurel wreath at her feet because she's a mixed-race Black woman who has "made it." We have to consider how she made it, why she made it, what power she has accrued, who gave her that power, and what she does with it. In other words, how do we hold the complicated and even harmful aspects of her persona while also celebrating her strides? Is this even feasible?

Like so many artists who look like her—like Nicki Minaj—Cardi wouldn't have the career she has if she weren't light skinned. There is a long and cruel history of light-skinned Black women and non-Black women with racially ambiguous looks capitalizing on Blackness as a means to an end (money, fame, social power).

If she were darker, one wonders what the reception and perception of Cardi would be in pop culture. Would she, like Azealia Banks, an equally problematic Black woman, become a pariah? What would the narrative become? Well, one doesn't really wonder; one knows. She wouldn't be on the pop charts. She wouldn't be doing Pepsi commercials. All the things that make her refreshing—her loudness, outspokenness, hoodness, aggressiveness—are things that have been historically denigrated in darker-skinned women.

There's a white gaze fixed on Cardi B that she can't shake off. It looks at her and she has to look back. There's a paternalism that white media greets her with, because white media, somehow, doesn't understand that who she is in public is not necessarily a shtick. Performative, yes, to the degree that all celebrities perform in public—but not a shtick.

On one of her first major late night interviews, with Jimmy Fallon, she was asked to explain some of her best "catchphrases." Fallon would hold up a cue card, maybe with the word "Eeeow," maybe with "Okkurt," and Cardi would say it, sling some funny little one-liner. The crowd would laugh. I laughed, too, but it was laughter born from a familiarity, an understanding, a connection. I couldn't help but wonder what fueled the mostly white audience's laughter, watching Cardi perform Blackness in a way that was tangible and comfortable for them, that was predicated on the very idea that everything about her—even the way she speaks—is a novelty.

Throughout the trajectory of her career, I've wondered whether Cardi's refusal to perform creates a doorway through which the white mainstream can comfortably (from their perspective) step into appropriation. Cardi is both authentic *and* performative, which is tricky to clock if you aren't well versed in the art of performance. The white gaze rarely understands the nuances of performance, allowing white audiences to embrace the fantasies of racist stereotypes *through* her, laughing at her when they think they're laughing with her.

Can white audiences only make sense of her by turning her into a minstrel, or by politicizing her in ways she never asked for? Yes. And they do, to the detriment of those who would want to lovingly (or hatefully) critique her. Because when we talk about the power of celebrity, we must also talk about accountability, and how to hold those who wield that power accountable. Sometimes, it feels as though power, as it exists now, is tantamount to a decided and intentional and concerted lack of accountability. Cardi is easily swept up into the white gaze as palatable, because of her light skin, because of the ease with which she is made a caricature. This results in a mainstream audience that uses this as a pass to not engage with the implications of her stardom in a meaningful, critical way.

Over the course of her stardom, Cardi has done and said several cringeworthy things. A brief list: calling women (in this case Black women) "roaches," using the r-word about herself and others, selling dangerous "flat tummy" teas on her Instagram page, defending Offset for referring to his haters as "gay," having an employee who posted a transphobic meme on her Facebook, using transphobic slurs herself, shooting a music video for "Bodak Yellow" full of orientalist stereotypes, posing as the Hindu goddess Durga, hosting a thirty-five-person maskless Thanksgiving dinner during a pandemic. By the time this is published, she will have probably done/said something else worthy of being added to this list.

Cardi never apologized for her stigmatizing "I hope your fucking mom catch AIDS" comment. (Do you remember this, from a few pages ago, or did your mind gloss over it the way fans and the media largely did?) She never apologized for once calling a Black woman's dead child a monkey during a back-and-forth argument in her Instagram comments (the woman, a random commenter, had simply made fun of Cardi's teeth). On the roach comment, she explained on Twitter, "I called my OWN self a roach before, so stop it!"

"It's a word I use a lot, Bronx bitches use a lot, stop trying to make it into some racist shit." A dubious distinction at best.

And then there's the history of transphobia. There's the 2015 clip of her explaining what she would do if a man cheated on her. She says: "I'mma take him out, we gonna get drunk, I'mma get him all perced up and everything we gonna have a good time. Get him super twisted. Then bring a bitch around. We gonna have a threesome. And when he wake up he gone be like what the fuck? Because the bitch was a tr—y. I'mma be like yup. Yup we had a threesome with a tr—y. Yup, a tr—y sucked your dick."

There's the time a transphobic meme was posted to Cardi's Facebook account, a picture of someone looking out of a window with the text, "I hope nobody see this tr—y leave my house," followed by a series of emojis.

"I am a huge advocate for free speech but as long as it's socially acceptable to make jokes about trans people, to make and share memes disparaging & demeaning trans folks, trans folks will continue to be murdered & denied civil rights," tweeted Black trans activist, actress, and filmmaker Laverne Cox in response to the meme controversy. "There is an epidemic of violence against trans folks. It's not new. Lives are on the line."

Actress Angelica Ross also commented, tweeting:

"Black trans women are being killed because of jokes like this. These n—s are killing us to keep women like you @iamcardib from finding out. Cause you'll make fun of their manhood. This is how you encourage toxic masculinity that only ends up hurting you too sis! Apologize."

Cardi didn't apologize so much as offer up an excuse as a substitute for contrition. She claimed that a former employee of hers had access to the account, which she no longer had access to.

"I appreciate @iamcardib addressing the issue and taking responsibility like a boss," Ross responded. "The next step is taking the opportunity to teach the entire industry why this shit is unacceptable and will not be tolerated any longer. THAT would be allyship in action. Cis solidarity sis," the actress tweeted.

Since these incidents, as Cardi has grown more political, she has made gestures toward allyship, or at the very least gestures toward explaining herself. In February 2020, Cardi came out in defense of Zaya Wade, Dwyane Wade and Gabrielle Union's daughter, who had recently come out as trans and had been attacked and misgendered online by rappers Young Thug and Boosie.

"I understand that they just don't be understanding certain shit, please try to understand," Cardi said on Instagram Live. "Because sometimes you will be wanting people to understand you," she said. "So try to understand somebody else. Especially when it is a child." To Zaya, she offered: "Speak your truth. Speak your truth, and educate."

Later that year, Hulu released *Love, Victor,* a teen drama about a queer teenage boy navigating high school and his sexuality. Cardi B is mentioned in passing on the show. Someone tweeted about the irony of her getting a positive shoutout, given her past homophobic and transphobic comments.

"How the fuck am I homophobic or transphobic?" Cardi tweeted on June 30, 2020. "Have you been to a Caribbean island where you really see homophobia! Have you dealt with a parent that can't accept you for your sexuality? I said some ignorant things b4 that [I] apologised for & educated myself on it don't mean I'm [homophobic]." In Cardi's mind, perhaps the preoccupation with her past controversies was unfair because it made no space for recognizing the ways in which she had grown as a person.

She added, "Ya keep using that same 1 video that I apologize for over & over again to call me homophobic & transphobic but never post about the ones where I support the LGBT community which are multiples and the multiple tweets I posted in support.

"And I don't support the LGBT community because I have 'gay fans' I support because of the confused feelings I had growing up on is it normal to like girls? I support because I know how hard it was for my gay cousin to come out to his very strict Dominican family. I support because I know the pain my cousin from my mom side which is a Trans have a fucked up relationship with her dad for years! I support because I seen the transitions &

the feelings my glam team having during their time with they body transition & my sister."

A lot of these explanations make sense and seem genuine. A lot of them also read like deflections. Two things can be true at the same time.

As a cis woman, it's not really for me to forgive or absolve Cardi of these transgressions. I'm glad that she said something, but I wonder if it really matters, and how it could matter more. Minaj, similar to Cardi, has what some may call a problematic history and what others would call a history of homophobia, transphobia, and rape apology. A thread in their feud, drummed up by fans, has been who is the more problematic of the two, an aspect of the fan beef that to me largely misses the point of calling out and calling in.

Again, the question. What does it mean for Cardi B, a self-professed "regular degular shmegular girl" from the Bronx, to be consumed by the mainstream? It means that women like her have a reference point, a representative, but what her representation means for them remains to be seen. These girls, girls like Cardi, aren't on Jimmy Fallon spelling out how to say "Eeeow" to chuckling white audiences. Their Blackness, their hoodness, isn't always greeted with applause. They are not performers. If they perform at all, it is, in a sense, for themselves—for each other.

But Cardi's performance has a wider audience, wider

implications. Her body, her face, her voice, her life have been gobbled up by the masses as the ultimate feel-good underdog story. After that's over, I wonder, what's left? I'm not trying to paint Cardi as some tragic figure, that's far too easy, and she has demonstrated far too much autonomy for that.

And so Cardi B hasn't just been problematic, she's been straight up transphobic, and it isn't really for cis people to absolve her of her transphobia, should she be absolved at all. In absolving her, there's also been a tendency in conversations about her colorist and transphobic comments that gesture toward infantilizing her—"She's from the hood, she doesn't know any better."

The implication here is that girls like Cardi—girls from the hood, girls with thick Bronx accents, girls who strip, girls who grew up poor, whatever—aren't capable of grappling with these issues, aren't capable of being challenged or critiqued. When Cardi B says, "I'm a boss, you a worker bitch," what is she saying? What is she saying that she doesn't even realize she's saying? And what, implicitly, does she know? That wealth isn't necessarily the key to liberation?

You can't say Cardi is smart and then say she's dumb in the same breath. Cardi is intelligent, she has the capacity to reject the paradigms she perpetuates. You can bop to "Bodak Yellow" and acknowledge this at the same time, at the very least. People can transition from ignorance to understanding. But for them to do so, there's an imperative need for us (me, you) to recognize when we ignore ignorance because it is convenient, easy, and comfortable. There's a spirit of laziness in this approach that is so consistent and inherent in a society built on hierarchies. We need to push against that laziness.

When we ignore Cardi's transphobia in the name of reifying the same practices in racism and sexism that we abhor, that we are trying to break away from, we are buying into this symptom of laziness created by white supremacist culture. We need to resist that. Not expecting more from Cardi buys into a raced and classed assumption about her capacity to learn, grow, and do better. And thus, by some extension, an assumption about everybody else like her (including ourselves).

There are people who go off daily about the ills of colorism and transphobia and stan Cardi B. I'm not saying you shouldn't stan Cardi B. But how can you be interested in dismantling and deconstructing these things if you're not interested in acknowledging them, on some level, in the culture you consume? There's a discord we're pretending isn't there.

I say all of this (all of it) to say that Cardi has made me think a lot about what accountability looks like, what growth looks like, what power looks like. At times I have not known what to do with problematic Black women. Transphobic Black women. Colorist Black women. Violent Black women. But everyone—everyone—is problematic. Some, of course, more than others. To recognize this is not to absolve a person of their sins, to say their bullshit is acceptable or above reproach. It's simply a way of moving toward looking at them, and then ultimately yourself and the world you inhabit, more honestly. Usually, honesty is the catalyst for growth.

I think it's OK to acknowledge that there are some people whom we've put up with simply because we like them, and those we haven't because we don't. I think women like Cardi should be given room to grow and evolve. I also think they, and the structures of power they unknowingly represent, should be challenged constantly.

Critiquing structures of power that we all live under is not the same thing as critiquing a person. We must constantly try to tear down current structures that aren't working for any of us, even while offering individual Black women grace. There are people we will give the benefit of the doubt to because we assume (incorrectly) that they've had less access to the information and institutions that would prevent their problematic behavior. And there are people we give passes to because it's easy, because the things they do or say are offensive, but they don't directly offend or affect us. This is messy, and uncomfortable, but it's the truth, and maybe by acknowledging it we open ourselves up to navigating feelings around problematic people we *don't* like with more nuance. What would the world look like if we demanded more of each other? Of ourselves?

When I saw, for the first time, the video of Cardi talking about "tricking" a man into having sex with a trans woman, I realized Cardi's casual weaponizing of transphobia implicated me. Allyship can be performative. It can be selective. Therefore it demands rigor and sincerity. I understand the inclination to be cynical about it, or to be lazy, or to be willfully uninformed, because that's easy. But easiness always breeds difficulty, in the end.

In the past few years, there's been a lot of discussion about "cancel culture," particularly the so-called harm that it has wrought on highly visible people. Cardi herself has talked about how she is "uncancelable," as though cancellation, whatever that even means, is ever the goal of calling someone out. Indeed, it's rarely even possible with people who have accrued enough power and social capital. And so the goal, always, is accountability, because holding people accountable ensures that their mistakes, malicious or well-meaning, have less of a likelihood of happening again. Calling people out, or in, need not be seen as an inherently bad thing. In many ways it is an act of care. We can apply this thinking to Cardi. We can apply it to ourselves. We can interpret calling out as a loving act—*I want you to do better, I know you can do better. I'm going to call you out on your shit and, in doing so, I'm going to call myself out on mine.*

Like all of us, Cardi exists within a system. She suffers under the system, but she participates in the system as well. Her success is positioned to us as a fairytale, an underdog story, a feminist triumph, by picking and choosing the things about her that are convenient to that narrative. This picking and choosing collapses all that she is—inspiring, disappointing, flawed, evolving, helpful, harmful, violent, healing, and so problematic.

Harriet Tubman

Harriet Tubman: 1911. Library of Congress, Rare Book and
Special Collections Division, National American Woman Suffrage
Association Collection.

Girlhood

Whenever I think about Black women, and freedom, which is constantly, I think in images, particularly the images of us that have made indelible impressions on me and have stuck with me the longest. I conjure these images up easily:

Angela Davis stands at a podium as she gives a speech in Madison Square Garden in 1972 in an effort to raise money for legal expenses. She's wearing a lavender blouse with big bell-shaped sleeves. Her afro is full, and round, light shines through it, resembling what could only ever be described as a halo. She is standing behind a three-sided bulletproof-glass shield.

A picture I first saw when I was ten or eleven years old of Mamie Till Mobley, the mother of Emmett Till, standing over her only son's coffin with a look on her face that seems to vibrate with pain.

Brooke Xtravaganza in *Paris Is Burning,* skipping down the beach in a bright yellow swimsuit as she declares, giggling, to the camera, to the world, "I am as free as the wind that is blowing out on this beach!"

Whitney Houston in a glaringly white tracksuit with red and blue accents, standing in the middle of Tampa Stadium in 1991, singing what is and perhaps always will be the most moving rendition of the American national anthem of all time. I think about how she raises her fists in the air as she hits that final, crescendoing note. A crowd of 73,813 fans burst into resounding applause.

I see that last image, a vibrant snapshot in my mind, and then my thoughts begin racing forward to what this image means, the context that swirls around it. Like the fact that Robyn Crawford, Whitney's confidant and lover, was standing just 12 yards away from her as she sang. And then I think about how Whitney and Robyn grew up in Newark, New Jersey. I think about how Whitney was four years old and at home during the riots throughout Newark in 1967 and how after they were over, her parents packed the family up and migrated to East Orange for a better life. I think about how her great-grandmother, Susan Drinkard (Dutch, African American), and her great-grandfather, John Drinkard Jr. (Native American), migrated from Georgia to Newark in the early 1940s, also for a better life. Then I think about the life that Whitney lived. I think about how she died.

For me, these images make up a story not just of a life but of what that life means in a greater context. These images, of Angela, of Mamie, especially of Whitney, bring up vital questions: How do Black girls find freedom? Where do they go to find it, to feel it, uncomplicated and uncompromised? Whitney Houston was once the most famous and celebrated woman in the world, and yet, was she free?

These moments, these flickers of freedom, are always complicated and compromised by unseen forces and unheard stories, and perhaps that's what makes them so beautiful. When Whitney Houston sings the national anthem in that iconic video, she's not just a pop star singing the national anthem. She imbues the song with more meaning than anyone who isn't a Black woman could retain. She sang of "The land of the free and the home of the brave" even as she grappled with the reality of having to hide parts of herself, of playing the role of America's sweetheart when she was beautifully, complicatedly, anything but. At least, that's my interpretation. That's what these images mean to me.

I've made a career writing about images and what they mean, so sometimes it feels impossible not to go down this wormhole of meaning, of considering what these things represent. It's the representation of things that make up the world we all exist in. I find that I go on these tangents especially with the icons of my millennial childhood, the symbols who formed and informed my understanding of what it means to look like and to be seen as a Black woman.

When I was a little girl, around eight years old, the Spice Girls were at the height of their fame. I don't have many vivid memories about my childhood, a byproduct of trauma, but I remember the almost all-encompassing love I had for Melanie "Mel B" Brown. I remember *insisting* while standing on some school playground some afternoon that if we were going to "play the Spice Girls," I *had* to be Scary Spice.

It wasn't even as if anyone else really wanted to be her. She was Black. She was "Scary." But there was a sense of pride, a sense of urgency, in claiming what felt tantamount to an earthly right. I didn't associate her with all the things that were traditionally supposed to be associated with her. She didn't frighten me. She emboldened me. What made her "Scary" were all the things that I loved about her and that made me want to be more like her. She was loud, gregarious, opinionated, had the most amazing mane of big, curly brown hair, and a love of conspicuous fashion: cheetah and tiger prints and high platform shoes. She was dynamic. She was *weird*. Looking back, I think perhaps what drew me most to her was the fact that she stood out *because* she was Black, not in spite of her Blackness. And, wow. That felt like a *good thing*.

I'm a Spice Girls collector. Not of memorabilia, but of moments. I have a private archive of all my favorite performances, fashion looks, and interviews. A few years ago, I found one interview they did on a Dutch talk show in 1997, at the height of their pop culture dominance, when their debut album *Spice* became the biggest-selling pop album by a girl group ever. The clip on YouTube begins abruptly. There is an initial cacophony of sound that reveals itself to be voices battling for dominance— the Spice Girls are sitting on a stage before a small studio audience yelling "No! No! No!" while the host, some white guy, beckons for a backstage surprise to come out.

Five white people in costume skip onto the stage. They're dressed in ensembles that conjure up a mix of Renaissance court jesters and elves in Santa's workshop, with ruffled collars, big gold earrings, and feathered hats. To complete the look, and the insult, they are all wearing Afro wigs, exaggerated red lipstick, and Blackface. The crowd cheers. The costumed people smile and wave at a few nervous-looking blond-haired kids in the audience. Mel B shakes her head in disbelief.

"I don't like them. We don't like them," she says, gesturing behind her. "I think they shouldn't paint their faces. You should get proper Black people to do it. You shouldn't paint their faces. I don't think that's very good . . . This is the nineties!"

The host offers a thin explanation for these costumed people dressed as Zwarte Piet, the mythical Christmas companion of Saint Nicholas. He says, "It's the tradition. That's the culture." Then he tries to be funny. "It's Winnie Mandela. Hello, Winnie!" And then, again, "It's the culture."

"Well, you should alter the culture," Geri "Ginger Spice" Halliwell chimes in.

I don't think it was until I watched this clip, at age twenty-seven, that I ever considered what Mel B represented outside of what she meant to me. I never thought about what it was like for Mel B to be the only one like her in the Spice Girls, and in the pop cultural landscape as a whole. To be biracial, Black, unabashedly loud and opinionated, to wear her hair natural, to navigate being both a role model and a commodity, a face on a tin of lollipops or a Spice Girls doll box. And what was it like to have to call out Blackface in that room full of fans, with those minstrels behind her, while her group mates offered what was ultimately a feeble defense?

I didn't think about those aspects of Mel B because I was a child, but also no one—not her fans, not the media—seemed to be thinking about those things because it's more expedient and comfortable to revel in the image than to revel in what the image means. The thing about the lack of representation that we don't talk about enough: it breeds desperation. It flattens nuance. It makes you unconsciously starved for kernels of recognition, imperfect as they may be.

Mel B was my first experience with this yearning for recognition, significant in that she rose to fame at a time when I was feeling particularly unseen. But the Spice Girls glamorized tokenism or, if not tokenism, this idea that one exceptional Black girl is all the representation that one needs. In a 1997 *Guardian* profile written by Katy

Weaver, they presented themselves as a "type of paradise" and a "community." Geri explained: "We're a community in which each one of us shines individually, without making any of the others feel insecure. We liberate each other. A community should be liberating. Nelson Mandela said that you know when someone is brilliant when having that person next to you makes you feel good."

This opportunity to "feel good" by association, this idea of being part of a utopic feminine society where what makes you different makes you special, was part of the appeal of the Spice Girls, and especially Mel B. In looking back, though, a question comes up about why I and so many other Black girls like me identified so keenly and perhaps desperately projected meaning onto this model: this ability to "belong" while still being different.

In the decades since the Spice Girls' world-dominating popularity has waned, Mel B has spoken more candidly about the precariousness of the space she held in the culture. She's spoken about being urged early on in the creation of the girl group to straighten her hair, and about how in 1998 she was bombarded by racist letters from neighbors in a small village where she bought herself a post-Pepsi-sponsorship-money mansion. In a 2020 interview, she revealed that she and she alone was asked to leave a luxury store while shopping with the other Spice Girls.

"Of course, all the girls had a go at the assistant because they were so shocked," she explained. "It's pretty awful to think I wasn't actually shocked because if you are brown then there's always a part of you that expects some confrontation."

As a kid, there was something aspirational about who I thought Mel B was, because there was something about her that seemed to effortlessly transcend the reality of these expectations and make me believe that I could somehow transcend them, too. (It's the things that look effortless that often take the most effort.) As an adult, in considering that the opposite may have been true, there is something cathartic, affirming, and complicating about Mel B.

But pop culture is where we go to find complications and, more importantly, contemplate how these complications make us feel. If we want it to, it can provide us with the tools with which we can begin to figure ourselves out. Wanting to be Scary Spice at recess was a part of this process: it helped me to form for the first time impressions about my sexuality, my mind, my voice, and who I wanted to be in the world. It was the start of a life of contemplation in an effort to understand who I was, and also who the world believed me to be.

Growing up, my crushes were Orlando Bloom, Ben Whishaw, and Joseph Gordon-Levitt. This is astonishing to me. Occasionally, the memory that I had a crush on *Orlando Bloom* makes me giggle wildly to myself. Because, what? It also makes me a little sad. Back then, I wasn't able to fully interrogate why I had these crushes on men who are so the opposite of my type now, that it was a kind of unconscious conditioning.

Frantz Fanon wrote in *Black Skin, White Masks*, "It is on that other being, on recognition by that other being, that his [man's] own human worth and reality depend. It is that other being in whom the meaning of life is condensed." In other words, to be human is to be seen, to be seen is to exist. In a racist society, this yearning manifests in ways that we are not even conscious of. What does it look like, for so many Black girls, to search for recognition in a society that both implicitly and explicitly refuses to acknowledge that you exist?

I never asked myself why I thought I desired the very type of man that Hollywood had reminded me, time and time again, did not desire me. It wasn't even as if I was swirl-obsessed, in need of the validation of white dick. (I've never seriously dated a white man and, if presented with the opportunity, I'm not entirely sure that I would—the dynamics are too fraught for me.) I was in need, perhaps, of a different kind of validation. The validation to imagine new worlds for myself. I was projecting myself into mainstream culture's mandated equation for romance. Me, plus some basic white man, equaled happily ever after. Fitting the equation, maybe, gave me the hope that this proximity could give me access to the world of the seen.

In her excellent essay "All Alone in Their White Girl Pain," cultural critic Safy-Hallan Farah writes, "I think visibility as an emancipatory concept is much about autonomy. It is about groups and individuals having the power to actively build their public image instead of being the passive object of discourses shaped by others."

Visibility, then, could be described as a gesture toward a specific kind of freedom: the freedom to define rather than be defined. Or, perhaps more specifically, the freedom to assert that you are undefinable because you are a human being. But visibility, or inclusion, or diversity, or any of the other buzzwords that have been used to approximate the solution to a lack of intentionality and care when it comes to images of the marginalized, is tricky.

During a 2015 talk at USC, Angela Davis said, "I have a hard time accepting diversity as a synonym for justice. Diversity is a corporate strategy. It's a strategy designed to ensure that the institution functions in the same way that it functioned before, except now you have some Black faces and brown faces. It's a difference that doesn't make a difference."

In other words, representation alone will not save us, no matter how much we want it to, because most representation that exists now is designed to placate instead of liberate.

When I was growing up (and even now) I often grappled with the ecstatic drumbeat of pain that comes with wanting to feel seen when you cannot even see yourself. I'd go searching for myself in other people, in the movies, in TV shows, in social media, in the cultural landscape that unfurls itself before you on tablet and laptop and phone screens every day. Later, when I became a culture critic, writing about film and television, I developed a deeper kind of neurosis around this search, because it was now a part of my work, which made navigating the distinctions in how art made me feel—and what I had to say about it—so confounding.

In 2014 I had the opportunity to interview a director whom I've admired my entire life, Spike Lee. I was familiar with his work in the same way that I'm familiar with the work of Steven Spielberg or James Cameron. Which is to say, his work, his persona, his aura, felt ubiquitous in my life, fully synonymous with the concept of cinema in my mind. The legend of Spike Lee, the enormity of who he is and what he represents, seemed almost oppressive to me as I made my way one summer morning from my home in Jersey City, New Jersey, to his 40 Acres and a Mule headquarters in Fort Greene, Brooklyn, to speak to him about his latest film, *Da Sweet Blood of Jesus*.

I'd seen the movie a few days before and hadn't liked it. The film was a modernized remake-slash-homage to Bill Gunn's underground classic *Ganja & Hess*, an experimental vampire love story. Where *Ganja & Hess* was challenging and captivating, *Da Sweet Blood of Jesus* was plodding, unwieldy, and rough around the edges in a manner that was neither charming nor compelling to me.

I remember arriving at Lee's company headquarters and waiting in a spacious, gallery-like room with walls that were decorated with large, vibrantly colored posters of Lee's past films: *Do the Right Thing*, *Bamboo-zled*, *She's Gotta Have It*. As I took in the posters, those monuments to his genius, I nervously gripped a notepad with questions hastily scribbled across it. My questions sought to somehow mitigate my less-than-fond feelings toward *Da Sweet Blood of Jesus* by emphasizing my admiration and overall respect for Lee as a trailblazer, an artist who had opened doors and opened minds even in his imperfection as an artist.

I was sent for and led up a flight of stairs and into a small office, where Spike sat on a rolling office chair in a corner by a desk and, on a small two-seat sofa opposite him, sat the stars of the movie, Stephen Tyrone Williams and Zaraah Abrahams. I situated myself, took out my phone, and started the voice recorder. I don't remember the first question I asked. I do remember, though, that the energy rolling off of Spike was palpably feisty—something I had been told to be chill about by my editor and some film critic friends. In my naive twenty-three-year-old mind, I figured that if you build a career like Spike Lee, you get a pass to be a little caustic. I was prepared for that and didn't mind it.

One of the first questions I asked that day was something along the lines of what made him decide to do a remake of *Ganja & Hess* in the first place. "I don't like to use the word remake," he said, "I think reinterpretation is a better word." Fair enough.

"And *Ganja & Hess* was directed by . . . ?" he added.

I blinked. "Bill Gunn."

"And starring?"

"Marlene Clark. Duane Jones," I stuttered.

Spike stared at me, smirked. I was being quizzed.

The rest of the interview continued with this energy. I would ask questions of Spike, of the actors, and yet the whole time I felt I was somehow being scrutinized, sized up, and tested. It was an unnerving, frustrating feeling. I wondered if I was projecting or reading too much into things, but my intuition told me otherwise. I doubt that Lee even registered, really, that he was making me jump through hoops in order to get him to engage, but I felt it acutely—this sense that my knowledge, my expertise, my reason for being in the room were being challenged.

That feeling of not being taken seriously is one I've often carried with me as a woman, and especially a Black woman, who writes about art and culture. The interview with Spike was one of my more visceral experiences of that feeling, but it had been there most prevalently on trips to film festivals like Locarno and the Toronto International Film Festival where (mostly white) male critics treat conversations about cinema like some sort of duel, a fight to the death, a contest to see who knows more.

There aren't many Black women in this game, and it's systemic—a USC study from 2018 found that 80 percent of film critics who reviewed the top films of the year prior were male and almost all were white. Another study, by San Diego State University that same year, revealed that

83 percent of all female film critics were white. Studies to show us things we already know. There is a dearth of Black female critique on film, TV, and culture, which is absurd, given that Black women are some of the biggest contributors to pop culture.

And yet, the Black woman critic has not been considered to have expertise, especially and particularly in texts that don't involve her identity. And, conversely, she has been made to feel like her opinion is invalid because it is informed by her Blackness, by her womanhood. She is accused of being too emotional, too personal, too subjective in her analysis, as if the act of processing art could ever be truly objective anyway.

Experiencing art is a personal journey, informed by so many things that have everything to do with identity. In 2018, I wrote a piece for *HuffPost* titled "White Film Critics Love 'Three Billboards' the Way They Love Their Racist Uncles." The headline was, admittedly, a little spicy, but the thesis of the piece stood: I'd read so many essays written predominantly by white male film critics that dismissed or altogether ignored the blatant racism of the main character (played by Sam Rockwell) whom we, the audience, were encouraged to root for. The character's racism was positioned as merely a personality quirk, one that simply added color and complexity to the character. (We learn early on that he brutally beat an innocent Black man prior to the events of the story.)

Art does not necessarily have to be uplifting, but I think it should be honest. Movies that present racism as an individual's character flaw and not a collective, cultural, systemic reality are simply lying. Which is a strange artistic choice, because the truth is and has always been so much more interesting, even when presented in fiction. As someone who has often had to write about art that was intentionally never intended for me, I've become acutely sensitive to this kind of dishonesty.

After my piece went live, I remember receiving a DM from a white male critic whom I'd always respected. "This isn't entirely fair," he said, referring to my assertion that it was easy for white critics to root for this character because they were already used to dismissing or ignoring the casual or overt racism of the people in their lives. This isn't fair, he said. And what was I supposed to say to that? You're right? I know? Forgive me? These exchanges, these microaggressions, are designed to make one feel like an outsider.

Top five worst feelings I've ever felt: sitting in a cramped, darkly lit karaoke room, the only Black woman among mostly white, male film critics. It was 2012, the night before the official launch of the Toronto International Film Festival, my first year covering the festival. I was new, and nervous, and excited to have been invited to this critic meetup, excited to step inside the room, which smelled of B.O. and tequila.

I remember sitting there as the opening instrumentals of Jay-Z and Kanye West's "Niggas in Paris" began to play. I remember watching several of my white colleagues sing along, carefree, rapping out the lyrics with

the ease of people who had sung the song to themselves numerous times.

"Ball so hard muh'fuckas wanna fine me. But first niggas gotta find me."

It wasn't just the fact that all these white people were giddily saying this word right in front of me. What was jarring and painful was that they weren't oblivious to my presence: they were fully aware that I was in the room, that I was watching. And that's what made what they were doing all the more violent and violating. I left and ran into the karaoke bar's waiting area. I sat, I think waiting for and wanting someone to stand up for me, to disrupt the festivities, to run out and comfort me. No one did.

I had never felt this particular kind of isolation nor the debilitating fear of that kind of isolation. I remember wondering if this is what navigating these spaces, this industry as a Black female critic, would always be like. Not taken seriously as a professional. Not taken seriously socially. Constantly trying to navigate how and when and whether to ever, ever talk about race, in my life and in my work.

"Debate me" culture is prevalent on Film Twitter. White male critics or just straight up trolls will subtweet you, neg you, and try to bait you into defending not just your opinion but your right to have an opinion. But I'm no longer interested in writing in defense of myself. This is a distraction. And the distraction, if you give in to it, will leave you constantly editing yourself, questioning yourself, punishing yourself for not knowing more. I'm no longer interested in knowing everything, a boring concept. I'm far more interested in a life of constant learning. "Debate me" leaves no room for that.

Before I came to the realization of how toxic "Debate me" culture is, every interaction I had both online and in real life felt highly choreographed. All my energy went into proving that I was meant to be here, so much energy that there was nothing left for me to feed back into myself. I wonder how many other women, how many Black women in particular, feel this as well.

In *Playing in the Dark*, Toni Morrison writes that "Statements . . . insisting on the meaninglessness of race to American indignity, are themselves full of meaning. The world does not become faceless or will not become racialized by assertion." Neither will the art that we consume, no matter how hard some of us will it.

In my living room, right above my television, there long hung a framed image of four Black girls. The girls are all silhouetted in a neon haze, their brown skin glows blue-Black as if illuminated by moonlight. They are smiling. Their arms are around each other. They are dancing. They are also singing. I know this because the image is a still from a movie I first saw when I was twenty-four, *Girlhood*, or *Bande de filles*, a French movie released in 2014. Directed by Céline Sciamma (who also directed

Portrait of a Lady on Fire), *Girlhood* tells the coming-of-age story of Marieme (Karidja Touré), a teenage girl growing up in the projects just outside of Paris.

It's a film that, for whatever reason, has been a catalyst, a framing device, for how I think and write about representation. It was at the center of robust and rigorous debate when it first came out—Black women writers like Fanta Sylla and Morgan Jerkins (more recently in her book *This Will Be My Undoing*) have written about its fallacies, its failings.

There's a moment in the film, the moment captured in that framed still above my TV, when Marieme and her friends joyously sing along to "Diamonds" by Rihanna. *So shine bright, tonight, you and I, we're beautiful like diamonds in the sky.* The first time I saw this scene, during a screening at the Toronto International Film Festival, I burst into tears. Watching that two-minute scene felt momentarily like stepping through a portal into a little pocket universe of Black girl joy that I, up until then, had never seen or experienced cinematically in such a specific way. I was moved; something inside me felt activated, if only for the length of the song.

I left the screening, went straight to my hotel room, and wrote some giddy and enthusiastic review. I commended the film for capturing "the unique process of growing up that so many Black girls . . . must navigate." The movie is perfectly good. But reading the review now it's so obvious that my review was in response to that one, singular scene: four dark-skinned Black girls in a moment of unmitigated, uncomplicated joy, a small respite from the onslaught of trauma, abuse, and toxicity their characters endured outside of that small, blue-lit hotel room. Which is to say, I fell into the trap of gratitude. The trap of feeling so grateful for even a momentary view of ourselves in art that we fail to fully interrogate the art for what it is.

Could that two-minute scene of the girls singing along to Rihanna make up for the fact that the film as a whole boiled down to yet another voyeuristic story of hardship, poverty, and trauma? And what does it mean that, in spite of this, I still cling to that image, cling to it enough to frame it? Gratitude that comes out of desperation is dangerous, as is the urge to define something as important or radical or "necessary" merely because it exists. There's a danger in contemplating moral urgency without at first contemplating the art.

Not long after my review, I had the chance to interview Sciamma herself for the Black film site Shadow and Act about writing and directing the movie. I remember meeting her in a very beautifully decorated room somewhere in upper Manhattan. I remember thinking she looked very sharp in a white shirt and blazer. I remember her being nice.

She told me how she'd been inspired to make the film by the Black teen girls she'd seen hanging around at the malls of Paris, how they had intrigued her, how they had represented to her the spirit of the "youth of today." She said the decision to have her lead character,

Marieme, be played by a Black teenage girl was an intentional one. "I really wanted to put a stone in the traditional French [coming-of-age] narrative, but with a very contemporary character never seen on screen," she explained. "And I very much wanted it to be a Black girl."

I asked Sciamma about her position as a white writer and director, about the white gaze, and about her thoughts on assertions that the film doesn't truly capture what it "means to be a Black girl" (these were the words I naively used).

"Obviously I can't tell the story of what it is to be a Black girl, but maybe I can tell something else. *Girlhood* is not about what it's like to be a Black girl, it's about what it's like to be a girl, and she can be Black." She continued: "But that's the paradox. It becomes a paradox. Because there is very few representation. Suddenly the movie has a new responsibility. That's a lot on my shoulders. I knew that when I was going for it. But I mean, I didn't know how messy it could get, because . . . I'm making this universal, and I decide that my character, who represents the youth of today for me, can be Black."

"She's no longer universal then," I offered.

"But she should be! It feels crazy, but I believe that in five years, there'll be other movies like this, and this one will be one of many. That is my hope."

What feels crazy, for me, is wanting to reach back in time to that conversation and push harder, force

Sciamma and perhaps more importantly myself to truly unpack that statement. As seemingly innocuous and well-meaning as the statement "in five years, there'll be other movies like this" was, it had nothing to do with meaningfully contemplating what it meant for her as a white, queer, woman filmmaker to claim the Black girl experience as "universal" or to suggest that if it isn't, it should be. Universality is another trap, another secret pathway to appropriation and miscommunication.

Literary critic Parul Sehgal wrote in a 2020 *New York Times* review of the controversial novel *American Dirt* about the argument that "imagining ourselves into other lives and other subjectivities is an act of ethical urgency." She added, "The caveat is to do this work of representation responsibly, and well." Part of that responsibility is truly grappling with the fact that historically, there is very little about the Black woman experience that we get to keep or interpret for ourselves, including our girlhood.

There is a misconception, as critic Nijla Mu'min has written about extensively, that there are no coming-of-age stories about Black girls. There is, in fact, a cinematic canon spanning decades and including films like *Just Another Girl on the I.R.T.*, *Crooklyn*, *Eve's Bayou*, *Akeelah and the Bee*, *Precious*, *Pariah*, *Yelling to the Sky*, *Beasts of the Southern Wild*, *Half Nelson*, *Solace*, *Selah and the Spades*, and *The Hate U Give*. These films, especially those written and directed by Black women, add something vital to a tapestry of Black girl coming-of-age stories. They add specificity.

But only a certain type of authenticity. So many mainstream white girl coming-of-age stories, even now, are imbued with a charged levity in ways that Black girl narratives aren't. So many of them explore a mundane, suburban ennui, a bored dissatisfaction with life, conflicts that never transmute into the kinds of trauma centered in Black girls' stories. At least, that is what it always felt like.

Another image I think about often: a video that went viral in 2015. In it an unarmed fifteen-year-old Black girl clad only in a tie-dye bikini is roughly manhandled by a police officer. (Complaints were made about a group of Black teens at a pool party in McKinney, Texas, and police arrived.) The officer pulls his gun on her. He drags her to the ground. He violently restrains her by sitting on top of her as people look on. She cries, she calls out for her mother. This two-minute clip is emblematic: of the lack of care for Black girls, the violence against them, the constant disruption of the mundane joys of girlhood. Like a pool party.

Which came first: videos and moments like this, or the movies that traffic in our trauma? I think about how I grew up with absolutely no coming-of-age movies about Black girls, let alone dark-skinned Black girls, that resonated with me. How there were no dark-skinned Zendayas or Amandla Stenbergs during my adolescence. How the teen movies I grew up on—*10 Things I Hate About You,*

She's All That, Bring It On—never actually centered on Black girls as the love interests or heroes.

How the absence of these cultural touchstones seemed to imply and even emphasize a societal lie: that Black girls don't get to be girls, they don't get to fuck up and discover, to be bored and be stuck in boring lives, that their childhoods do not exist, that they simply spring, fully formed, into a precarious womanhood, a lie that in a small way validates and perpetuates the sexual violence and indifference Black women face on a daily basis.

Making Marieme and her friends Black in *Girlhood* wasn't inconsequential. In using these young Black teens as a conceit, as part of an exercise in re-creating the traditional French banlieue but with a "contemporary" feel or, it seems, with edge, Sciamma was able to explore the themes she said that she cared about—freedom, destiny, conforming versus not conforming—by projecting these ideas onto Black bodies, which, whether many white filmmakers are conscious of it or not, intrigue them because they cannot understand how these bodies can exist on screen. Or they've never considered that they can before. So the film, the show, the novel, whatever it is, becomes a way for these white creators to implicitly explore their own bias, their own guilt, their own inability to understand. *That's* interesting. But only if they're willing to acknowledge it.

To be a writer is to constantly be learning, publicly, to present a public record of a changing mind. Looking back at the transcript of my conversation with Sciamma makes me cringe. I have compassion for myself, but I still *cringe*. I feel uneasy and naked when I consider my deference, the immaturity of my politics and praxis, the way I can see and hear myself utilizing the talent that so many Black women cultivate: the ability to deftly assuage white women of their guilt or their ignorance for the sake of their comfort. I'm happy to say that I've let go of that talent. It never served me.

Representation is always framed as important and necessary, as if the only value of representation lies in its very existence. This leads to complacency. Representation is not—and should not always be—positive. The point of representation is not to only represent easy things, "good" things. Its existence is not valuable or necessary simply due to some moral obligation of the art.

And I think, again, about that image in my living room of the four girls. Images, like words, are powerful. They mean something. What does it mean for me to cling to an *image* of girlhood so strongly, an *image* out of context, out of time? What does it mean, in fact, to actually "see me" on a big screen?

Sciamma's insistence on the power of making the "Black girl" an everywoman in a movie landscape where stories about Black girls are already so few and so fragile comes back to me. The teenage girl in McKinney, Texas, comes back to me. I think about the images prior to her abuse that we didn't see, that we'll never see: her and her friends lounging by the pool, gossiping about boys they like at school. Doing cannonballs in the water. Playfully splashing each other. Making noise. Being girls.

This duality, the before and the after, the image of the Black girl dancing and laughing versus the Black girl suffering, is a tension, a complication I'm constantly thinking about when I watch the stories of Black girls on screen. Because of this tension, the Black girl *can't* be every girl. She shouldn't have to be. The exclusivity of our stories, and the ability to interpret them, sometimes feels like all we have.

I used to think that to be free meant to be unburdened. Now, I'm starting to think that maybe it's something else. Something I've been meditating on: How can people imagine new worlds for themselves if they are never given the tools to do the imagining?

I rewatched *Girlhood* for the first time in five years recently. It was a very different experience. The images moved me, but not the way they had before. It was not a bad experience; indeed, it gave me something more substantial than the initial glee of watching the "Diamonds" scene so many years ago. For the first time, I watched the scene on the TV in my living room with all the nuance of time. For a moment, the image of Marieme and her friends dancing on the screen synchronized with the image of them framed above the screen, one perfect shot, one specific context, echoed. The movie continued.

I recently took that framed image above the TV down. Not because I don't still love it, but because it no longer holds the meaning it used to for me. And it doesn't have to. I'm grateful for the exhilaration I felt when I first saw it. But I'm no longer grateful for images of Black girls simply because they exist. I've replaced the picture with a large white-framed mirror that bounces light all over the living room, a trick to make the space look bigger than it actually is. My boyfriend thinks it's odd, but what I absolutely love is that now, when I watch movies on the TV, I can see myself.

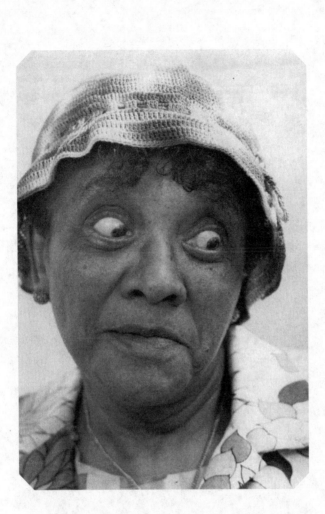

Jackie "Moms" Mabley

Jackie "Moms" Mabley in her stage persona from
a guest appearance on the *Smothers Brothers Comedy Hour*
television program. CBS Television. May 31, 1968.

Strong Black Lead

Melancholy is exhausting. I'm thinking here of the weary feeling after I've dragged myself into the shower to wash off the sludge of a week of sleeping instead of bathing, and then dragged myself out of the bathroom and into my bedroom to find something to wear in the piles and piles of clothes strewn about the floor (some dirty, some clean, it's impossible to tell, and it doesn't matter at this point). I pick parcels of clothing up and I sniff. Good enough.

Good enough. It's all I can do to not dissolve into the floor, staring into the closet, focusing on the sensation of breathing so that I don't forget to breathe, or the feeling of the soles of my feet against the wood floor so that I don't collapse into myself. And I am tired. Tired of the effort it takes to function, to think, to focus on anything but what feels like an overwhelming, bone-deep need to be sad and, more than that, to wallow in that sadness.

Sometimes it's hard to know what to do with an unsettled mind once you've acknowledged that you have one. At one time, especially during the first-person-industrial-complex boom circa 2015, I wrote a lot about being depressed, coming out in my writing at varying stages of mental health with varying diagnoses. Then I began to question who or what it was helping, to bare my pain and my trauma to strangers on the internet.

I felt uneasy exposing myself, even as I recognized that talking about my mental illness, creating an open dialogue for Black girls like me, was important. Even with all the messiness that exposure entails, the anxiety and the fear of judgment, talking about and writing about my reality has been helpful. I tell myself that it's important for someone like me to be honest about my melancholy. I believe that I'm helping someone, somehow. At least, that is the hope.

I know, especially in the age of people as content, that vulnerability can be seen as currency and nothing more. For me vulnerability is a part of survival. I would rather people think I'm messy, cloying, don't have my shit together, am looking for attention and sympathy, than believe that I am totally fine. "Totally fine" comes with unrealistic expectations that I cannot and do not wish to meet. As a Black woman, I have enough unrealistic expectations to worry about as it is.

Our identities shape the way we navigate the world, and how the world navigates us. When I think about myself, I think, "I'm Black (first), I'm a woman, I'm a writer, and I'm mentally ill." I abhor that last part, that it even comes into the equation, but it feels so embedded into the fabric of my life that it seems wrong *not* to acknowledge it as a part of my identity.

But as much as I try to accept it, my neuroses, my trauma, can be draining on a soul level. When I was younger, I remember thinking that if I had certain things—a job, a partner, a beautiful place to live—my self-loathing and my sadness would magically disappear. Now, I have a lot of those things and I've realized that depression is annoyingly unconditional. It doesn't depend on the external. This is obvious, and basic, but it's a horrifying realization for me all the same.

I thought my lowest moment came in 2018 when, around three a.m. one weekday, in the throes of an es-pecially bad bout of depression and anxiety, I had flip-pantly tweeted something that had alarmed some of my followers, something along the lines of: "I really need people to pray for me. I'm trying my best to stay alive." In my sad haze I thought this was innocuous enough, though perhaps a touch morbidly cryptic, not the kind of tweet you should post before letting your phone die and crying yourself to sleep. And yet, chile, that's what I did.

I don't know who specifically put in the call, but they

did, and I was woken up a few hours later to frantic text messages and calls from friends, coworkers, and family asking if I was alright. I felt terrible. Knowing I had freaked so many people out wasn't even the worst part. Neither was being placed on leave from work because I might be a danger to myself or others. The worst part was hearing the loud, ominous bang on my apartment door. Then having to watch my boyfriend of four years stand bleary-eyed and confused in our foyer wearing only his boxers, forced to greet four police officers and an EMT (all white, all male) there to do a welfare check.

The little gang poured into our apartment, seeming to fill up every corner of the space, take up all the air. I felt like I couldn't breathe. I tried to hide it, to present a veneer of bemused calm as one of the officers asked me if I was OK. Yes, I answered. Was I planning to hurt myself? Anyone else? No, I answered. Did I feel like I needed to go to the hospital? I was really, truly fine, and this was all a misunderstanding, I insisted.

This whole exchange couldn't have taken that long, but somehow it felt as though it took an eternity to get them to leave. I remember parts of the conversation that felt aggressively irrelevant—one cop commented on the layout of my apartment, complimented the white Moroccan rug in the living room. I cannot remember how and on what note they finally left, but when they did, I felt the overwhelming rush of air entering my lungs again and had to immediately sit down on the floor. The distinct energy of several strangers I didn't know, all carrying guns, invading my apartment, still hung in the air.

I felt an awful and thick shame, the kind that sticks. I felt so bad that it was impossible for me to look my boyfriend in the eyes for several hours. Part of the shame, I think, was knowing that even though I had insisted that I was fine, I really and truly wasn't. The other part of the shame was confronting the reasons I wasn't fine. I was having disturbing recurring dreams about the man who sexually assaulted me. I wasn't sleeping. I was binge eating and gaining weight, which only intensified my self-loathing. "I wish I would die, I want to die" was a phrase that sprang to my mind at least several times a day, a constant mantra so familiar and consistent that part of me had learned to just ignore it, let it fade into the background. Things were not OK, I couldn't lie my way out of the pain of that.

I was on leave for three months. I wish I could say that during that time I got my shit together. I can't. It was during this period, after all, that I made my first suicide attempt, an experience that even now I haven't fully processed and still haven't found the words or the strength to write about. What I can say is that I watched a whole lot of television, listened to a whole lot of Cardi B, tried to inundate myself with pop culture so as to lose myself in something other than my own pain for a while.

The problem was that this mountain of depression and anxiety hit me hard just as the world was entering what felt like a period of chaos, a period in which the realities and horrors of white supremacy felt heightened. I was being inundated with images of Black death at home, then inundated with them at work, where I had to write openly and candidly and constantly about the pain and pathos of a racist society. Many times, before I could even fully process my feelings of anger and sadness, I felt compelled to bare those feelings, work out those emotions, for public display. I had to write through pain, out of necessity, when all I wanted to do was shut down.

For the longest time, I did not know what to do with this. I did not know what it meant or how to change it. There was no road map to dealing with my pain, after all. When I was coming of age, I did not have access or exposure to depictions or conversations about dealing with mental health, Black or white.

There were not many examples in my life of Black women crumbling, struggling, reaching out for help. My family held a lot in. I didn't see my mother cry until I was well into my twenties. I was alone most of the time. And when I went searching in pop culture, all that came up for me was the concept of being "strong." Be strong. Suck it up. Figure it out. Get over it. Get it together. Stop being messy. Why are you crying? It's not that deep. What's the matter? Why can't you articulate what's wrong? Perhaps because nothing, in fact, is wrong? Be strong.

Calling Black women "strong" is a silencing tactic. Let's

start with that. "Strong" is a weak offering, a label often intended as praise or encouragement or admiration but that subtly implies: *Black girls, every ill of the world that you must contend with—the racism and misogynoir, the transphobia, the colorism, the fatphobia, the hyper-sexualization and sexual violence, the invisibilization, the trauma, the disregard—all of this you were made to endure.* "Strong" says that life for Black women can only be an aggregation of pain. That we were made for pain. "Strong" suggests that it is part of the natural order of things for Black women to remain all alone in their pain even as they lift entire communities up. "Strong" is a fucking myth.

And yet it is a myth that has permeated so deeply and so widely within the culture that even the images of Black women that in more recent times have tried to subvert and challenge this trope have, in a sense, also perpetuated it: Pam Grier's ass-kicking Blaxploitation chick in *Coffy*, the take-no-shit characters Okoye and Michonne portrayed by Danai Gurira in *Black Panther* and *The Walking Dead* (respectively), Viola Davis' quietly suffering housemaid Aibileen Clark in *The Help*, Kerry Washington as Olivia Pope on *Scandal*, who always has it "handled," whose PTSD after being kidnapped and tortured is played merely as a plot device rather than an integrated part of her character.

If these women crumble, it's only for a moment, it's only for show, it's only to highlight and emphasize their strength when they regroup and get it together. Their ability to bounce back without lasting repercussions is what we're expected to focus on, not necessarily their pain. I don't think any of the depictions mentioned, or countless others like them, are inherently bad, without value, without nuance. But I'm just interested by how their strength is almost always presented as an attribute that better allows them, ultimately, to prop up other people rather than solely just themselves.

Portrayals of Black women truly grappling with their mental health on screen in mainstream culture are precious and rare. Nola Darling on Netflix's *She's Gotta Have It* or Molly on HBO's *Insecure* opening up to Black women therapists about their troubles with commitment. Or Mary Jane on BET's *Being Mary Jane* dealing with the aftermath of her best friend's suicide. These examples are sporadic and sparse, but they open up new ways of seeing oneself, new possibilities for healing.

It's not enough simply seeing someone who resembles you; you also need to be exposed to experiences, realities, stories, that echo your own. The key thing about representation, if done well, is that it blocks isolation. It allows viewers to understand that they do not exist in this world alone. It forces those with different experiences to acknowledge that other people do exist.

I avoided the 2020 Christmas special of the TV show *Euphoria*, titled "Rue," for weeks after it came out. *Euphoria* was cute, if flawed, but when I saw the preview for the episode I knew immediately that something about it would break me, and it did. It was the type of television that I hadn't seen in a while: a quiet, intimate, melancholic character study that forces you to think of your own weaknesses as someone else's are being laid bare. I saw so much of myself in Rue (played by Zendaya)—depressed, self-loathing, and caught in a loop of self-sabotage and addiction as a way to distract from underlying trauma and inner pain.

There are two moments in the episode that reached out to me, that struck me so hard I had to press pause and have a good, long cry. The first was when Rue, a seventeen-year-old suburban drug addict who's just had a relapse, sits at a diner on Christmas Eve with her sponsor, Ali (Colman Domingo). She says to him:

> The world's just really fucking ugly, you know? It's really fucking ugly, and, um . . . Everybody seems to be okay with it, you know? The anger. The level of anger. Everyone's just out to make everyone else not seem human. And I don't really want to be a part of it. I don't even want to witness it.

And the second moment, where Ali says this to Rue and yet I felt like he came directly and specifically for my edges:

> Your only hope is a revolution. But a real fucking revolution—inside and out. But you gotta see it through. You can't half-ass this shit. You just have

to commit to it, every single day. And know that you can always do it better, and be better. Because who knows? One day you might succeed.

One day you might succeed.

The episode ends with a single shot, a slow zoom held on Rue's face, furrowed with contemplation. To me, it's the face of a person processing the realization that the choice to give up on themselves or keep trying is, ultimately, completely up to them. There's something terrifying about that. And beautiful.

What is being a Black woman if not having to constantly hold the reality of the terror and beauty of your experience at the same time?

An obvious question comes up: Does being Black make you more likely to be depressed? I believe there's a lot of intergenerational trauma passed down within the diaspora through the ages that we haven't even begun to unpack yet. I also believe that being Black, being queer, being marginalized in any sense adds a new tenor, a new layer to mental illness. In other words, my Blackness doesn't make me depressed, but being Black in this world can be depressing.

There isn't a lot of substantial research about the role that mental illness plays in the lives of African American women. This is unsurprising. We know that anxiety, depression, phobias, and schizophrenia are more prevalent in African American women than they are in African American men, white men, and white women. We know that queer Black women and transgender women are at a higher risk of depression than any other group, that they attempt suicide at higher rates as well. And yet statistics are never as telling as lived experiences, as individual stories.

Blackness is filled with so much joy, too. Black joy is effervescent, and in my moments of clarity, when I can hold it up to the light and watch it sparkle, that truth is truly transformative. But I think, in some sense, the ex-uberance of Black joy springs forth from Black despair. Collectively, we made a way out of no way, created music and food and language and dance and art as a means of survival, as a medicine that the entire world benefits from. And so, I believe in a sense that the world-shifting energy of Black joy is echoed in intensity by Black despair. I don't know if there's anything else quite like Black despair, that personal, historical, collective, diasporic pain.

When I first entered one of my recent dark spells of depression, there had been an onslaught of Black death back-to-back-to-back. Philando Castile and Mike Brown and Eric Garner. There had been the 2016 presidential election. There had been the Muslim ban. There had been Parkland. There had been Pulse. And then there was Nia Wilson, the eighteen-year-old Black girl stabbed to death by John Lee Cowell in July 2018.

Something I couldn't stop thinking about after her death was Nia's sister Letifah Wilson, describing to the press her last moments with her sibling:

"She's just yelling my name, 'Tifah, Tifah, Tifah,' and I said, 'I got you, baby, I got you. Just calm down,' because she has real bad anxiety."

Letifah, Nia, and their sister Tashiya were on their way home after attending a family gathering. They used Oakland, California's BART train system to get home (the same BART system on which Oscar Grant was murdered), which always made Nia anxious and uneasy. The train pulled into their station. And as they walked off the train, Cowell ran up, stabbed Letifah in the neck, then slashed Nia's throat. According to Letifah, he paused for a moment, watching as Nia bled to death, then ran away. Before he was eventually sentenced to life in prison, the case against Cowell would be suspended in order for officials to conduct an investigation into his mental health.

Amid the pain and horror of the attack, yet another reminder of what it means to be a Black woman in America, a part of me couldn't stop thinking about the significance of the panic, the trauma of what the Wilson sisters experienced, and the panic, the trauma that all Black women experience. I couldn't stop thinking, also, about what it means to be a Black woman living with mental illness, with depression and anxiety, and how incidents like Nia's death are not symbolic of this experience but rather concrete evidence of the fact that to be a Black woman in the world is to hold, somewhere deep in the pit of your stomach, a sense of fear, a knowing that at any moment your dignity or your safety or your life could be compromised.

So many Black women know the stress, as sociologist Eve Ewing put it on Twitter in July 2018, of walking home at night and "feeling the danger from all sides." The danger often feels inherent, tied so tightly to the unique concoction of racism and misogyny that goes with being Black and being a woman. It's a fear, Ewing explained, that we constantly carry, that "[builds] up in our bodies, killing us like a poison if we don't first face punishment for simply being alive."

We know the feeling deeply and intimately, just as we know the feeling of being the only one in an office or classroom of white faces, just as we know the feeling of our demeanor being misconstrued as threatening or aggressive, just as we know the feeling of having to "keep it together" for our spouses, our children, our families because nobody else can (or will), just as we know the feeling, the psychic stress, of being a Black woman in a world that is burning (and has always been burning, despite what some may think) and that doesn't seem to care about you.

We know the feeling, but so many of us do not have a name for what we are experiencing. And when you cannot name the thing that torments you, it makes the thing all the more terrifying.

For Black women, mental illness takes on so many confusing shapes because we often designate ourselves as caretakers, as fixers, as keepers of all the shitty parts of life. That's why we're so "strong," and why we have to be. From generation to generation, we're made to feel as though for every experience of trauma we've overcome, there's always another one around the corner, so we need to stay vigilant.

Mental illness manifests itself in many ways, and it affects everyone uniquely. Meditating on the murder of Nia Wilson, a murder that left me once again clinging to the familiarity of my bed, I realized that my fear of being in the world, of taking up space, is deeply tied to being a Black woman.

Depression may take root in your head, but it's compounded and intensified by the realities of everyday life. Worry and madness can live in the body, manifesting as aches in the muscles, mind-numbing migraines, relentless insomnia, memory loss, gastrointestinal issues that stay with you long term. I've experienced this all. I grew up with a mother who was in a constant state of worry and fear—fear about finances, fear about the precarity of being an immigrant in America. There was always an air of anxiety in our home, this dread that another shoe was constantly about to drop.

I know that fear found its way to me, I know that these things are inheritable—just like the hypertension and heart issues that run in my family that led to my mother being on the brink of death one day not long ago because her heart just stopped beating, briefly, before she was revived. That's what it feels like, sometimes. Like my heart has stopped beating.

When I was at one of my low points in 2018, staying inside my one-bedroom apartment that I shared with my partner for weeks and weeks on end, retreating from the world seemed like a logical and easy way to cope with the idea of existing in the world. But Nia Wilson's murder created a tiny but profound shift. It concentrated my mind on how the anxiety of taking up space as a Black woman has so many knotty threads. I went from blaming myself to understanding that the stressors outside of me had far more impact than I gave them credit for. Black women are killed in America at a higher rate than women of any other race. Trans Black women are killed at an even higher rate. Violence against Black women exists on so many planes, from the physical to the emotional to the spiritual.

I think about the Wilson family, the trauma and anxiety piling on top of Letifah Wilson's grief. I think of her saying: "I was her protector, and I feel like I didn't protect her."

The helplessness of these words, the helplessness of not being able to protect Nia from the violent hatred of this world, is a helplessness that resonates with me deeply. And I do not really know what to do with it all except to give a name to what torments me. My Blackness is not the problem. My sadness is not the problem. My anxiety is not the problem. The problem is the constant specter of white violence and its consequences, the reality of it, the fact that I'm made to feel like I'm crazy because it makes me feel crazy, the fact that I must fight to exist as white violence continues to exist and nobody seems to care.

Narratives are the stories we tell ourselves to make sense of the nonsensical, to give order and explanation. There's this narrative that Black people don't believe in mental illness, a narrative that suggests that many people throughout the African diaspora are raised to pretend the idea of mental illness doesn't exist, or is at the very least a problem most sufficiently treated through prayer to a Christian God. This is the kind of mythmaking that distracts us, that oversimplifies a story, that robs us of a sense of understanding of our own histories.

It's true that African Americans are less likely to report or seek help for mental illness, as a 2018 study by the U.S. Health and Human Services Office of Minority Health reported. A 2019 study conducted by the *Journal of Community Health* found that from 2001 to 2017, the rate of death by suicide for Black girls rose by 182 percent.

To suggest that these numbers prove that Black people don't know or don't care about mental health and wellness tells only half a story. Throughout my entire mental health journey, I didn't feel cared for, heard, or seen until I finally began seeing a Black woman therapist. That's real. There is a specific lack of care for Black patients in the medical world that can be life threatening. Black people have less readily available access to healthcare, and Black women particularly are less likely to have their pain taken seriously by physicians.

There isn't simply a stigma within the diaspora that

impedes treating mental illness; the overwhelmingly white mental health and wellness worlds stigmatize Black women in turn. In other words, there is a complementary narrative of denial. When Black women do take the time to seek help, they often find a hostile or doubting audience of medical professionals. Here is a narrative in which white people pretend that white supremacy does not exist, that it has no bearing and no impact on all of our lives.

When people who have lived in war zones experience trauma, depression, PTSD, no one questions why. That war is hell, that it manifests itself in the human psyche in all kinds of horrible ways, is an accepted fact. But in America, we're not allowed to blame white supremacy, a material force in the lives of Black and brown citizens that has produced an ongoing war of terrorism—sometimes state-sponsored—against them. To point to white supremacy as the thing fueling the flame of spiritual and mental illness is to point to the phantom that nobody will engage with, that nobody with any real power in this country will admit exists.

So we figure out ways to cope. Sometimes it's retreating from the world. Sometimes it's hardening ourselves to the world, mistaking a near-constant awareness of danger for an existence creeping toward normalcy. I know we deserve more. I know, for damn sure, that Nia Wilson did.

I want her to rest in more than peace, more than power. I want her to rest in freedom. Freedom from burdens, freedom from expectations, freedom to feel things deeply and messily and destructively without having to worry about how the expansiveness of our emotions inconveniences other people. I want us to be free of the fear that sadness is all we'll ever know.

Recently I came across this, something I scribbled out in my Notes app during a spiral, dated November 9, 2019, 3:04 a.m.:

Will I ever have a normal life? Will I ever get better?

Symptoms

Lethargy, low energy, frequent naps during the day (at times mildly catatonic), insomnia/racing thoughts from 10–4am

Suicidal ideation "I wish I would die, I wish someone would stab me in the face, i don't want to be alive"

Thoughts of self harm "get the knife"

Negative thinking "I'm worthless, nobody loves me, I'm stupid, I'm trash, I'm ugly, I'm fat"

Obsessive thoughts about body/food-tortured about what to eat and when. Periodical bingeing late at night (McDonald's 5 nights in a row)-usual binge as mixture of comfort and punishment

Lack of interest in work, friends. Complete inability to focus. Severe procrastination. Difficulty completing simple tasks (cleaning, bathing)

Retail shopping-reckless/careless spending

Fear/anxiety about leaving home, long stretches of staying indoors (35 days straight)

Deep self loathing

I

"I feel I'm running out of time to be happy"

"I feel I'm running out of time to be happy."
Something inside me shatters when I remember the place of hopelessness I was in when I wrote those words. In a world that seems to revolve around the death of Black and brown people, this feeling of time running out is ever present, an albatross around the neck. This is what white supremacy wants, what it's always angling for, to crush the imagination, to quell the belief that we can be free of the prison of our own minds.

There are days when I have clarity, when I can wake up and blinkingly look around at the little life I've made in spite of everything—my incredibly loving partner, my cozy apartment, my caring friends, the privilege I have of being able to write for a living. These things are reminders: another world is not only possible, it *exists*. I've created it. It *exists* for Black girls, no matter what we're told to believe. This is the hope I hold on to. This is a knowing that I have inside of me, that I try not to forget: There is *always* time. Peace is coming.

Ida B. Wells

Ida B. Wells: Portrait from the 1893 book
Women of Distinction by L. A. Scruggs, 1893.

Free of Cares

I'm free, white, and twenty-one!

Between the 1920s and 1940s, this phrase was ubiquitous in Hollywood movies. It was practically a meme, a cheeky, snappy catchphrase, a declaration with which any glamorous white heroine—Norma Shearer, Ginger Rogers, Carole Lombard—could assert her independence. It was a signal to the audience: this was a young woman with a decided lack of fucks to give.

But take the shell off a sentence like that, "I'm free, white, and twenty-one!," and its ubiquitousness signals something else. It established an implicit truth, a collective but unspoken knowing in America: youth, possibility, freedom, these things were all within the domain of whiteness. And Blackness simply wasn't. When a white person used this saying, they were speaking about themselves as much as they were speaking about Black people, about the reality of America, a place where youth, possibility, and freedom were associated exclusively with whiteness.

In 1935, journalist Walter L. Lowe wrote of the saying in the *Chicago Defender*:

The expression: "free, white and twenty-one," conveys no doubt the following thoughts to the average white theater-goer: "I am white, therefore, bondage has no place in my life. I am white, therefore I am a superior person. I am white, hence I encounter no social or industrial discriminations." To the average person of color, the phrase: "free, white and twenty-one," as it is employed in moving pictures dialogues conveys the following suggestions or ideas: You are not white: you are, therefore, an inferior person. You are not white; you are not, therefore, entitled to social and industrial freedom.

Eventually, the phrase would be banned by the Motion Picture Association, apparently not so much because it was offensive to Black people but because, essentially, it was fodder for Cold War Russia to point out the failures of American democracy and capitalism.

The phrase died off. The reality of it, what it represented, of course, did not. The words echoed in Hollywood in images of white womanhood that were meant to assert their autonomies even as those images denied and ignored the reality of Black women's lives. I see "free, white, and twenty-one" in the careless entitlement of every character on *Sex and the City*, a show that I love. I see "free, white, and twenty-one" on the Instagram page of every independently wealthy white girl influencer with millions of followers and nothing to say. I see it in the casual cruelty of so-called Karens, who believe their entitlement is more important than Black folks' lives. And I see it in a video from January 6, 2021, of a white woman believed to be Elizabeth Koch from Knoxville, Tennessee (though she has since denied this, claiming it is just someone who looks like her). In it, she has just stormed the Capitol building with hundreds of white supremacist insurrectionists to protest Donald Trump's loss in the election. She's crying because an officer allegedly maced her. If she were Black, it's hard to believe that burning eyes would have been the worst of her injuries.

She looks at the camera and with sincere belief says, "It's a revolution."

I've always been fascinated by the white concept of freedom because, as a Black woman, as an immigrant from a colonized country from which millions of Africans were stolen and then enslaved, I've always felt that the white conception of freedom lacks urgency and honesty. The white conception of freedom declares "I'm free, white, and twenty-one!" and declares "It's a revolution!" without a true understanding of what either of those declarations means. Black freedom, on the other hand, calls this out, holds America to a standard it set for itself and yet refused to meet.

When I'm feeling anxious or overwhelmed, I like to watch Ken Burns' nine-episode epic *The Civil War* to soothe me. I don't know why. The documentary puts me in a semi-meditative state, a place of quiet contemplation mixed with horror. Sometimes, when I'm not in the mood to listen to novelist and Lost Cause sympathizer Shelby Foote drone on with his folksy stories about the bravery and pluck of the Confederate soldiers, or the decency of Robert E. Lee, I fast-forward to the parts—few and far between—where Professor Barbara Fields, the only Black woman expert featured in the series, gets to speak.

I fast-forward to her because her voice cuts through the bullshit. There's one moment, early on in episode one, where she sums up the precarity of the concept of freedom in America in a way so succinct and so matter-of-fact and so *true* that I often must pause just to process the words, let the simple truth of them wash over me like a cold wave.

She says, with slow deliberation, "If there was a single event that caused the war, it was the establishment of the United States in independence from Great Britain with slavery still a part of its heritage."

It is as simple as that.

And the simplicity of the statement is perhaps what makes it so profound, and so painful. What does freedom actually look like and feel like in a country essentially founded on a lie? In a country whose conception of freedom, from the start, was tainted and compromised and didn't have an overwhelming number of America's population in mind?

Growing up an immigrant, I was constantly made to believe that freedom was a thing that you had to earn, that you had to jump through hoops for. Freedom was presented to me as a privilege only afforded to those who could assimilate, keep their heads down, keep their mouths shut, work hard. And so my movements were limited. In the years before I became a citizen I did not travel without entering a state of panic that took days to leave my body after the fact. Borders terrified me. And so, from an early age, and even now, much of the way that I moved through the world was about making myself scarce, stifled, confined. Perhaps that's why I clung to pop culture so much—it gave me glimpses of another way to be in the world.

When I was ten and eleven and twelve, I watched reruns of *The Cosby Show* with a pious duty. (This was, of course, long before the show became fraught for me and many others, tainted by the ever-present reality that the man whose name is in the title of the show is an unrepentant rapist.) I felt, like so many others, that the fictional family members whose lives I was witnessing on screen were somehow my family, too. I had a mother and a big sister in the real world whom I loved, but the Huxtables were vital, a supplement to a home life where I spent most days after school alone with only the internet and the TV to keep me company.

I loved all the Huxtable kids, particularly Rudy (Keshia Knight Pulliam), whom I thought maybe looked a little like me (baby mustache and all), and studious middle-child Vanessa (Tempestt Bledsoe), because she reminded me of my big sister. I was intrigued by the second daughter, Denise (played by Lisa Bonet), the sixteen-year-old wild child. Denise was artistic, effortlessly cool, alternative in a way that I had never really considered a Black girl could be before. Her wardrobe, her hairstyles, her aura, even by the standards of the '80s and '90s, were completely unlike the standard teenage Black girl characters I'd seen on screen up until that point.

Each season of the sitcom Denise would show up in some weird, rapturous ensemble—a gray men's vest over a striped, puffy-sleeved purple dress layered loosely over baggy checkered pants and knee-high boots; orange slacks and an oversized button-down shirt the color of sea foam that looked fairly innocuous from the front, until she turned around to reveal that it was *backless*; an aquamarine velvet suit with comically, marvelously oversized black lapels.

Something was communicated here. Not simply through Denise's fashions but through her way of being, expressed by Bonet with a playful casualness that said, no matter what: *this is a young woman with a decided lack of fucks to give.*

I didn't know at the time that as Denise was attending Hillman College, dropping out, running off "to Africa" to work as a photographer's assistant, then secretly getting married and becoming stepmother to a three-year-old girl, Bonet herself was making similarly defiant, self-actualizing decisions about her life and her career.

In 1988 at the age of twenty-one, Bonet eloped with rocker Lenny Kravitz, then promptly got pregnant with her first child, Zoë, a decision that put her further at odds with Bill Cosby. They already had a contentious relationship. Cosby often found Bonet too difficult, too unprofessional, too hard to control. The pregnancy was just one of many perceived infractions Bonet had made. Also on the list: a graphic sex scene she had done with Mickey Rourke in a movie called *Angel Heart* and a (iconic) nude cover shoot for *Rolling Stone* magazine.

Bonet's pregnancy coincided with her stint on the Cosby spinoff *A Different World*, which showrunner Debbie Allen suggested at the time might actually be a "great thing" for the show. "To see a girl who's this upper class kid, having a baby, not married because she didn't want to be married . . . and the girls could root for her," Allen said in an interview for the Archive of American Television. Executive producer Cosby wasn't having it. The idea of Denise, rebellious though she was, becoming a teen mom was beyond the pale.

So Bonet left *A Different World* and returned to *The Cosby Show*. Her pregnancy was hidden. She stayed on for a few more seasons before eventually being fired in 1991 for "creative differences." I remember watching those later seasons as a tween, not yet knowing the behind-the-scenes story but still sensing a distinct resistance in the way that Bonet played Denise's later and final storylines, which saw her drop out of school and start a family—to her father's dismay.

While her father could only see her choices as risky, destructive, unruly, I could see Denise had an incredible ability to roll with the punches of life. She seemed to not only embrace chaos but *thrive* in chaotic situations. And more than anything, she seemed like the kind of girl who wasn't afraid to be exactly who she wanted to be. This was something I desperately aspired to. There was a quality, an attitude, to Denise that I was drawn to, a way of being that I wanted to try on. I didn't know quite the exact word for it back then, but later, I found it. Carefree.

There's an entry on Wikipedia that credits me as one of the first people to coin "Carefree Black Girl," back in May 2013, but the origins of the phrase are nebulous, more a collective dialogue. I feel we all somehow, synergistically, conjured up Carefree Black Girl together, in a moment when visibility was a central theme in internet culture. When *I* used it, it was in reference to a Tumblr blog called "Carefree White Girls," created by writer Collier Meyerson in 2011. The blog, populated with pictures of happy-go-lucky white girls like Taylor Swift and Zooey Deschanel living their best lives, aimed to critique "the ways in which popular imagery reinforces the deification of white womanhood."

"#Carefreeblackgirl" was a hashtag that, as it grew in popularity across social media, became a space for images of black women experiencing joy, living *their* best lives. Folks would use the hashtag to share selfies, as I had, or they would populate the hashtag with pictures of their favorite Carefree Black Girl inspirations. Blooming from the concept came a Tumblr account created by blogger Danielle Hawkins, a podcast by creative Quanna MC, and dozens of think pieces explaining who and what the Carefree Black Girl is.

If you image search "Carefree Black Girls" right now, you will invariably come across pictures of Black women who have some of the spirit of a Denise Huxtable or a Lisa Bonet. You may see groups of light-skinned, slim, able-bodied girls with curly 3C afros smiling unclouded, uncomplicated smiles. You may see flower crowns and crochet halter tops, wavy goddess locs and dream catchers, ankh necklaces and adinkra tattoos. You may see Solange, Zoë Kravitz, Willow Smith, Zendaya, Yara Shahidi. Early on, these were the images overwhelmingly associated with the Carefree Black Girl aesthetic, and what eventually drew the most critique. These images that suggested that the Carefree Black Girl had to be a certain color, a certain size, a certain socioeconomic background, a certain age, usually cis and able-bodied. Naturally, and rightly, this version of the Carefree Black Girl was questioned.

In 2016, writer Shamira Ibrahim wrote about why she was "over the 'Carefree Black Girl' label," citing the fact that the idea was ultimately limiting and also dismissive of the real, lived experiences and struggles of Black women, particularly those within the United States. She wrote:

> Ultimately, why do we want so badly to have that carefree label? What is so intrinsically better about it? Being a [B]lack woman is amazing, and I fervently believe we should celebrate that at every turn possible. It's also hard, and consequently difficult, to create a "carefree" space in a world where there are so many lenses boring down on us. And that's OK! It really is. We shouldn't feel so beholden as to pursue this carefree state of mind when what most people seem to ultimately seek is as much self-determination as possible.

I get this frustration, this disillusionment with the concept of "Carefree Black Girl" in this context, because I've had those frustrations myself. (It isn't lost on me, for instance, that my young mind was quicker to associate light-skinned Denise Huxtable with my early conception of carefreedom than brown-skinned Vanessa who, after all, infamously went to Baltimore to have big fun with The Wretched.) Ideally, to be carefree is to be free of cares, and to be free of cares is to, ultimately, be free of preoccupation with anything beyond joy, love, and tenderness. As a Taurus Sun, this is a concept that activates me. As a Black woman, this is a concept that I find difficult to actualize in my everyday life.

In the living/dining room/kitchen of my first solo adult

apartment, I hung a pennant (made by Rayo and Honey) that read in big black letters "CAREFREE BLACK GIRL." I remember seeing the pennant every day on the far wall of the room in the mornings before heading to work and feeling a kind of distance from those words, a chasm between me and what I thought they meant. The years between twenty-seven and thirty were some of my most anxious, most depressed, most lost. Never in my life thus far had I been so hopeless—about my immigration status, about my family, about my career, about whether or not I would ever be happy.

I felt, personally, as if there was something pathetic, even dishonest, about embracing this term, not only given its criticism but also given how often I did not necessarily feel carefree. I wondered, is hanging the pennant a lie or is it an act of care, of self-preservation?

Which eventually flows to the most urgent question: What does it mean to be carefree? And what does it mean, especially, to be Black and a woman and carefree? What does it mean to be carefree and be a queer Black woman, or a disabled Black woman, a Black woman of trans experience, a Black woman who responds to they/them pronouns? What does it mean to *claim* "carefree" when Black women at all intersections are not always afforded the privilege to walk through the world unbothered? Some Black women, many Black women, walk through the world with the kind of careful intentionality of one who walks on glass, acutely aware of the confinements of their existence in ways that others do not have to be.

As a label, is the Carefree Black Girl no better or worse than, for instance, the Angry Black Woman? How is one empowering while the other disempowering? And while something can be empowering, can it actually confer power? I think that in order to embrace freedom we must also acknowledge all the things that make us feel unfree. In being carefree, we must also be, as art curator and writer Kimberly Drew put it during a 2017 interview on the podcast *Another Round*, "full of care."

In a 2016 interview with Fusion, the actress Cree Summer, who for years played free-spirited Freddie on *A Different World* (a character created specifically to replace/reflect the energy of Denise Huxtable), spoke about the so-called myth of the Carefree Black Girl.

"I don't know a single black girl who's carefree because it ain't easy being a girl of color, period," she said.

God, I wish we were carefree. A lot of political things would have to dramatically change in this planet for a woman of color to be carefree. But I think what they mean by that is more of an aware Black girl, a conscious Black girl. The more conscious you are, maybe the less cares you have and maybe the more cares you have as well—it kind of goes hand in hand. Self-awareness and more self-love and also the ability to care for other Black women. It has something to do with being politically aware of where you stand on this planet and I think it has to do with not accepting the definition that's been given to you by designing yourself. I've always been a loudmouth that way. I've always been proud to be different, I've always stood out like a sore thumb and I always have not given a damn.

In saying "I always have not given a damn," Cree invoked what could be a motto of the Carefree Black Girl—aware, processing, learning, persevering, and not giving a damn.

Part of that work, for me, has been trying to better understand the stereotypes that have been used in the past to make Black girls feel "unfree." bell hooks wrote that "To truly be free, we must choose beyond simply surviving adversity, we must dare to create lives of sustained optimal well-being and joy."

I think claiming and reclaiming what it means to be free, what it means to be carefree and also a Black woman, with all that entails, is itself a kind of freedom. The act of acknowledging the precariousness of our existence as *well* as the joy, as *well* as our ability to imagine lives and futures for ourselves that go further than the parameters of those that have been foisted upon us by society, by each other, by ourselves.

I also think of Carefree Black Girl as a framework in which to think of the Black woman's place and function and contribution to popular culture. The Angry Black Woman, the Mammy, the Jezebel, the Strong Black Woman—they all, when it boils down to it, are Carefree Black Girls. If "Carefree Black Girl," as an idea, as a concept, can be dismantled and broken away into tiny, manageable parts, parts that by exploring we're better able to understand the whole, then such is the case for any label placed on Black women, whether self-imposed or not. I'm interested in how Black women embody and perform their identities, how decades of stereotypes and pop culture tropes and imagery in movies, television shows, and social media have informed how we think about and feel about ourselves.

So, "Carefree Black Girl" is, number one, a way of being but also, two, a way to analyze the culture. Call it the Carefree Black Girl gaze. Seeing Black girls in popular culture as they are, for what they are, is a more radical, free, and human analysis than relying on tropes and stereotypes. Carefree Black Girl is the absence of these things, the denial of them. A Carefree Black Girl is, conversely, free of labels.

They are femme, they are masculine, they rocks weaves, they are natural, they're spiritual, they are not. They exist, and their existence is both political and apolitical. They exist, and their existence itself is a kind of declaration of independence. They are free because they decide they are free. They are free, above all else, because they are human.

This is the utopic vision that I have, that I hold on to. But then, always, I come back to . . . *but what can a hashtag do, really?* That potential for this expansiveness still doesn't make it any less fraught, any less complicated. Black women have used social media and the internet as a tool to anchor themselves and redefine their identities for so long—hashtags like #flexinmycomplexion and #blackgirlmagic and #girlslikeus have shown the potential for Black women in the digital space to subvert and shift paradigms, to form community and resist perceived narratives and control their own. That, I think, is what #carefreeblackgirl did. And yet, sometimes, I can't help but contemplate the both-and of it all. The frailties and fallacies of the online world become clearest to me when I contemplate the potential for the spaces we carve out in order to affirm ourselves to be co-opted, corrupted, commodified, and branded. I don't always know what to think of this, what to do with it. I mean, look at the title of this book.

Reading Breonna Taylor's tweets, which date all the way from 2012 to 2020, to the day before her death, is like seeing the snapshot of a life.

On April 25, 2012, at 11:02 p.m., she tweeted, simply:

Young, Wild, & Free !

On April 2, 2018, she tweeted,

A week from today I'll be in Vegas living life care free . . . much needed and deserved, I can't wait.

On February 19, 2020, she tweeted:

I wonder what my life would be like if I never moved here from Michigan? Like what tf would I be doing right now? Where would I work? Would I have kids? Etc.

A few hours later, the same day, she tweeted:

> Why do I feel like all my life Since I've been able to work I've always been the one making sure folks straight & nobody has ever looked out for me the same way.

When I read these tweets, I see a regular, beautiful girl just trying to live a good life. That's all. And yet, she didn't know. She had no idea that a portrait of her painted by the world-renowned artist Amy Sherald would be on the cover of *Vanity Fair* magazine. She had no idea she would become a meme for being killed.

On March 13, 2020, Breonna Taylor, a twenty-six-year-old woman in Louisville, Kentucky, was asleep in bed when three police officers used a battering ram to break into her home in the middle of the night, on suspicion of drug operations. They shot into her body ten times. She was alive and left unattended for six minutes after being shot.

Initially, only one of the three officers, Brett Hankison, was charged, and only with three counts of first-degree "wanton endangerment." This, a Class D felony. A petty crime. The charges were only tangentially related to Breonna's death—they had nothing to do with the bullets that went into her body but rather the bullets that were wildly shot into the walls and doors of multiple other apartments in the building Breonna lived in. Ahead of the announcement of the decision, for which a grand jury deliberated for less than an hour, the state of Kentucky had declared a state of emergency. White supremacy, you see, lacks subtlety. It is dutifully repetitive, redundant, predictable. It can elicit the desire to sob and flash a withering eye roll at the same time. It is exhausting. It is disappointing.

One can't really, even, call white supremacy a disappointment. To be disappointed is to, on some level, have been expecting a different outcome. What's the word for the kind of disappointment that settles in your bones early on and stays there? The kind of disappointment that's battered and weary? The kind of disappointment that can be mistaken for complacency but is really, more accurately, a kind of numbness?

I felt profoundly numb in the moments after I saw news of the trial results trickle in. There was this strange, hazy feeling that hovered over me, like déjà vu, a surreality that made it hard to feel anything besides a kind of quiet awe. All I could think about was how, in the weeks after her death, Breonna had become a kind of meme on the internet. Infographics, hashtags, and illustrations of her abounded. Calls to "say her name" were everywhere.

"Anyway, arrest the cops who killed Breonna Taylor." This became a common refrain, repeated across social media in tweets, in Facebook posts, and Instagram captions. The slogan and other related memes were an almost ubiquitous part of navigating the internet's conversation about police brutality and white supremacy, as more and more people who had never meaningfully thought about these things before began to dip their toes into that discussion. The broadened conversation was great in many ways: online resources helped galvanize Black and non-Black people alike to educate themselves about race, sign petitions, donate to anti-racist organizations and GoFundMe fundraisers, and bring attention to institutional racism in America. But the popularity of that call for action also highlighted the ways in which Black death has been commodified, trivialized, and used as fodder for performative allyship.

Among some of the most common Breonna Taylor memes were these: A picture of the cartoon character Arthur from *Arthur!* captioned with "And I say hey! What a wonderful kind of day . . . to arrest the cops who killed Breonna Taylor!" Numerous sexy selfies (like a since-deleted post from model Duckie Thot) with the caption, "Now that I've got your attention, arrest the cops who killed Breonna Taylor." A tweet that read, "Drink water. Use seasoning. And arrest the cops who killed Breonna Taylor."

"Memes frequently operate as exemplars of larger trends, as well as stand-ins for cultural anxieties and ways to express and alleviate fears or other emotions through humor," writer Aja Romano explained in an article for *Vox* about the popularity of World War III memes after reports that President Donald Trump had ordered the assassination of Iranian general Qassem Soleimani. For many people, then, memes and internet humor are coping mechanisms, a way to process, an indication of what we're all feeling and how to feel.

And yet it must be said that, similar to the World War III memes, things get tricky when you consider *who* is posting and laughing at "arrest the cops who killed Breonna Taylor" posts. It's one thing for Black people to try to process their pain and grief over her death through humor, but what about when such memes are made for and/ or by white and other non-Black people who are not affected or implicated in the same way? What does it mean for a white person who has never engaged with race in a meaningful way, who has yet to take actions outside the internet to combat racism, to tweet, "If you want clear skin, arrest the cops who killed Breonna Taylor"?

Perhaps the most egregious thing I saw during this brief trend in calling for justice was an ad for an online fashion boutique that sold a #SayHerName collection of cheaply made tops, each named after a dead Black woman: the Sandra Top, the Breonna Top, the Aiyana Top (Aiyana Jones, a seven-year-old Black girl killed by Detroit police officer Joseph Weekley). Even Black death is commodified. And this commodification, this memefication, always turns Black death into a theoretical problem, an abstraction, rather than something real and true that reverberates through lives.

The nature of memes, after all, is that they are transient. They come and then they go. Turning Breonna Taylor into a meme, then, turned the conversation around what justice looks like for her into a temporary fad. As "arrest the cops who killed Breonna Taylor" got repeated over and over again, it became an abstraction, it began to lose meaning. Indeed, it ultimately had no meaning. There were people repeating the phrase in one social media post while calling for the abolishment of police and the criminal justice system altogether in another. So where do these people actually stand? And what did the use of these memes say about their "good" intentions?

The thing about social media is that it creates a structure wherein hashtags become valuable, memes become valuable, slogans become valuable, selfies become valuable, but the lives and souls of Black women don't. A hashtag alone is a hashtag. It isn't activism, not even if it is inclusive or acts to frontline people who have been marginalized for centuries. A hashtag must exist in the world. Work that begins and ends at identity, that gets you on a panel or a book deal but does nothing to actually shift paradigms and dismantle systems, is perhaps not really the work we should be focusing on anymore.

Some things I now know: Freedom has to be about more than being seen. Being seen is not a guarantee of being understood. And to be seen and misunderstood is perhaps the greatest plight of the Black woman. Without understanding, there is no care, no protection, no consideration. People can look at you and instead of a person they can see a symbol or they can see a void. And, if you are not careful, you may begin to look at yourself and see these things, too.

All this to say, visibility is not protection. Especially not on the internet, where there are algorithms designed specifically to oppress Black voices and Black faces and Black expression, where existing as a Black woman is just as precarious as existing as a Black woman in the real world, where your name becomes a call for justice and yet you get no justice, restorative or otherwise. The more visible an idea, concept, or person becomes, the more vulnerable it is to cooptation and commodification, dilution and misinterpretation.

Take, for instance, #SayHerName, a hashtag specifically created for Black women after the death of Sandra Bland, but then used by MAGA supporters in 2021 to memorialize Ashli Babbitt, a thirty-five-year-old white woman who was killed during the storming of the Capitol.

In *Algorithms of Oppression: How Search Engines Reinforce Racism*, Safiya Umoja Noble writes about how the internet is designed to uphold racism, explaining, "Algorithmic oppression is not just a glitch in the system but, rather, it's fundamental to the operating system of the web." If the internet is a shadow, a reflection of a real world, then of course it operates within the systems in "real life" that are similarly racist.

Facebook, Twitter, Instagram—these are platforms that I use or have used to connect with other Black femmes and learn more about liberation, and yet, I cannot ignore that though we try to carve out safe spaces for ourselves on these platforms, they are not safe for us. Their algorithms specifically target us, especially if we're dark skinned, fat, disabled, trans, queer. *Especially* if we actively call out their lax policies on racist trolls, their facilitation of white supremacist rhetoric and terroristic plots, their privileging of white, moneyed influencers, their rampant shadow bans of Black creators, their gatekeeping of information and ideas.

Perhaps the greatest tenet of the death cult of white supremacy is the normalization of brutality, the normalization of a system of valuing certain lives over others—that's exactly what algorithms do. And so I'm trying to find freedom outside of algorithms and hashtags, new ways to engage with community online that are about more than being seen. I want to be understood.

A few years ago, while scrolling through Instagram, I came across these words from my friend, a fellow journalist, Shonitria Anthony: "Been dreaming of freedom. Pondering: What does freedom mean? Have I ever been free? When was the last time I felt free? Will I ever be free in America as a Black Woman? Will my children be free?"

Her questions crystallized for me the fact that I, we, all want to be free simply and without complication. Without having to ask these questions of ourselves and our lives every day. Without coopting and misinterpretation. But freedom in this world, freedom in America, is complicated by design. And Black women are in a sense the answer to this complication.

In 1977, the Combahee River Collective, a Black feminist lesbian socialist organization founded in Boston, published a statement that encapsulates this idea for me, a truth: "If Black women were free, it would mean that everyone else would have to be free, since our freedom would necessitate the destruction of all systems of oppression."

That destruction, I think, begins with me. Destroying the concept of not being free in my own mind. Freedom is agency, and agency means being able to actively change the world you live in. They say if you smile when you're sad it'll make you happy, or if you stand with your feet wide apart and your hands on your hips, you'll feel more powerful. Not too long ago I had the thought, "What if I just pretended to be free?" Pretended, because I know that I'm not, none of us are, not in a world like this. But we can be.

And so I'm trying to catch tiny freedoms where and when I can. I hold on to them, like talismans of protection. I've realized that freedom is a shaky concept, ever changing, defined only insofar as one is willing to embrace it. Some moments when I've felt truly free:

- The first time I saw Josephine Baker dance.

- The feeling I had when I was sixteen or seventeen and discovered a movie I had never heard of before, or a TV show I had never seen, thinking I had this perfect secret, this thing just for myself, and nobody else knew it or would get it and feeling so cool in the way teenagers discovering the power of art for the first time always do.

- Being ten or eleven in my family living room, watching *Martin* on TV with my big sister, throwing my hands up and screaming in unison with Martin on the screen: *"Damn . . . Damn . . . Damn!"*

- The first time I kissed my partner, after a third date at the Sunshine Cinema in Manhattan; we saw *A Most Violent Year*, but all I can remember is his lips, and feeling held and truly loved, even then.

- Every time I've gotten to be in conversation with a Black woman I admire for my work—Viola Davis, Nikki Beharie, Regina King, Shingai Shoniwa, Yara Shahidi, Taylour Paige, Dee Rees, Ruth Negga, Shatara Michelle Ford—there's always a moment during these conversations where my perennial social anxiety dissipates, where I feel seen or I feel that I truly see them, and I can take a step back in my mind and think how lucky I am to be able to witness and write about Black women in an industry where so few of us get the chance to do so.

- On my thirty-first birthday, which occurred during the middle of the first wave of the COVID pandemic, sharing a five-minute toast with my friends via Zoom, feeling for the first time, through the screen, able to receive love, feeling for the first time like maybe I deserved it.

- The moment, a few years ago, when my abuser DM'd me a jovial message to "check in" on Facebook and I replied, "You no longer have access to me" and blocked them.

- Every single time I've ever allowed myself to imagine a new world for myself.

I'm going to continue to imagine. I'm going to dream, to create worlds in my mind where I am cared for, seen, heard, loved, and, yes, carefree. I'm imagining a world where Black women and girls like Breonna Taylor and Toyin Salau and Ma'Khia Bryant and Sandra Bland and Dominique Fells and Korryn Gaines and Brayla Stone and Natasha McKenna and Tatiana Hall and Miriam Carey and Merci Mack and *all Black women everywhere* can receive truly restorative justice, celebration, protection. I'm reaching out for a world where we value not just the representations of Black women but Black women themselves.

Whitney Houston

Whitney Houston talking to the audience before proceeding to perform "Saving All My Love for You" during the HBO-televised concert "Welcome Home Heroes with Whitney Houston" honoring the troops who took part in Operation Desert Storm, their families, and military and government dignitaries. March 31, 1991.

Acknowledgments

Thank you to the people who helped make the dream of this book a reality. Thank you to my family. Thank you to my literary agent, Connor Goldsmith, and my first editor, Kara Rota, who acquired this book and believed in it from jump. Thank you to my editor, Anna DeVries, and Alex Brown for the time, energy, and patience they put into helping me complete this project. Thank you to my therapist, Sacred Walker, who helped me heal so that I could write. Thank you to my assistant, Emily, who helped keep my head above water. Thank you to Michaela, Robert, Bozoma, Rebecca, Michael, Fariha, Janet, Yaba, Joi,

Devan, Akwaeke, Ashley, Sal, Jamie, Shaya, Genna, Sho-nitria, Joycelyn, Shirley, Arabelle, Roxanne, SaMya Over-all, and everyone else who reached out, checked in, and rooted for me while I was working on this book—especially in the moments when I could not root for myself. Thank you to Danielle and Kevin for reading my work and providing the loving, necessary critique I needed to go on. Thank you to Molly for your friendship and your optimism. Thank you to Keesean for the late-night talks, the laughter, the wisdom, and engaging with my writing in a way that made me feel seen and less afraid. Thank you to the love of my life, Gulab—your love, calmness, constant encouragement, support, and understanding over the last four years have meant everything to me. Thank you to anyone who has grown up with me on the internet and followed my journey from Livejournal, to Tumblr, to 2BG, to Instagram, to this page, this moment, and whatever happens next. I feel the loving energy more than you can know. Thank you, thank you, thank you to all the Black women who've come before me and who have inspired me to exist boldly. Thank you to my ancestors. Thank you to my God. Thank you to whoever reads this book.

Zora Neale Hurston

References

Introduction

to consider

Akil, Mara Brock, creator. *Girlfriends*. 2000–2008.

Badu, Erykah. *Mama's Gun*. Motown Records, 2000.

Broughton, Sarah, writer and researcher. *Josephine Baker: The First Black Superstar*. Forget About It Film & TV, for BBC Wales. 2006. Available on YouTube, November 13, 2011, https://www.youtube.com/watch?v=Ggb_wGTvZoU.

Finney-Johnson, Sara, and Vida Spears, creators. *Moesha*. 1996–2001.

Francis, Joe, dir. *La Revue des Revues*. France: Star Films Edition, 1927.

Junglepussy. *Satisfaction Guaranteed*. Vice Records, 2014.

Lee, Spike, dir. *Crooklyn*. 40 Acres and a Mule, 1994.

Riperton, Minnie. *Perfect Angel*. Capitol Records, 1974.

Simone, Nina. "'I'll Tell You What Freedom Is to Me. No Fear.'" Available on YouTube, March 4, 2019, https://www.youtube.com/watch?v=Y3YFrSlfZ9A.

#carefreeblackgirls

AARON PHILLIP

AÏSSA MAÏGA

ALICE COLTRANE

ALTHEA GIBSON

ANGELA BOWEN

ANGELA DAVIS

ANGELICA ROSS

ASSATA SHAKUR

BESSIE SMITH

BILLIE HOLIDAY

CARRIE MAE WEEMS

CHERYL CLARKE

CHERYLE DUNYE

CICELY TYSON

CLAUDETTE COLVIN

CREE SUMMER

DOROTHY DANDRIDGE

ELLA FITZGERALD

ERICKA HART

ERYKAH BADU

ETHEL WATERS

FLO KENNEDY

GABBY DOUGLAS

GABOUREY SIDIBE

GENEVIEVE NNAJI

GLADYS BENTLEY

GRACE JONES

HARRIET TUBMAN

IDA B. WELLS

JOSEPHINE BAKER

JULIE DASH

JUNE JORDAN

JUNGLEPUSSY

KASI LEMMONS

KELIS

LAVERNE COX

LIL' KIM

LINDA MARTELL

LISA BONET

LORRAINE HANSBERRY

LUPITA NYONG'O

MADAM C. J. WALKER

DR. MAE JEMISON

MARI COPENY

MARIAMA BÂ

MARIELLE FRANCO

MARSHA P. JOHNSON

MARY CHURCH TERRELL

MAYA ANGELOU

"MEL B" BROWN

MISSY "MISDEMEANOR" ELLIOTT

MISTY COPELAND

MOMS MABLEY

MUNROE BERGDORF

NAOMI CAMPBELL

NELLA LARSEN

NENEH CHERRY

NICHELLE NICHOLS

NIKKI GIOVANNI

NINA MAE MCKINNEY

OCTAVIA BUTLER

OCTAVIA ST. LAURENT

PAM GRIER

PATRICIA OKOUMOU

PHILLIS WHEATLEY

PHYLLIS HYMAN

POLY STYRENE

QUEEN LATIFAH

ROBIN GIVHAN

RUBY DEE

RUTH E. CARTER

SAIDIYA HARTMAN

SALT-N-PEPA

SERENA WILLIAMS

SHINGAI SHONIWA

SHIRLEY CHISHOLM

SKIN FROM SKUNK ANANSIE

SOJOURNER TRUTH

SOLANGE

SZA

TARANA BURKE

THANDIWE NEWTON

THELMA GOLDEN

TIFFANY HADDISH

TIFFANY "NEW YORK" POLLARD

TONI CADE BAMBARA

TONI MORRISON

TOYIN OJIH ODUTOLA

TRACEE ELLIS ROSS

TRACEY "AFRICA" NORMAN

TRINA MCGEE

VILISSA THOMPSON

WHITNEY HOUSTON

WILLOW SMITH

WILMA RUDOLPH

YARA SHAHIDI

ZORA NEALE HURSTON

Bodies
to consider

Farquhar, Ralph, et al., creators. *The Parkers*. 1999–2004.

Finney-Johnson, Sara, and Vida Spears, creators. *Moesha*. 1996–2001.

Goode, Karen R. "Bubbling Brown Sugar." *Vibe*, September 1998.

Hollywood Divas. Executive producers: Adam Reed, Leslie Greif, Carlos King, Anthony Sylvester, Todd Tucker, 2014.

Likké, Nnegest, dir. *Phat Girlz*. Outlaw Productions, 2006.

Lindsay, Kathryn. "Diddy Lizzo Twerking Instagram Live Video Controversy." *Refinery29*, April 13, 2020, https://www.refinery29 .com/en-us/2020/04/9684885/diddy-lizzo-twerking-instagram-live.

"Lizzo Addresses 'HATING' Her Body in Emotional TikTok Videos." *Entertainment Tonight*. Available on YouTube, December 11, 2020, https://www.youtube.com/watch?v=NBjcAf0ndU4.

Lizzo. *Juice*. 2019.

Lizzo. *Truth Hurts*. 2017.

My Next Guest Needs No Introduction with David Letterman. Season 3, episode 4, "Lizzo." Netflix, 2018.

"P Diddy stops Lizzo from twerking on live TV," available on YouTube, April 13, 2020, https://www.youtube.com/watch?v =XDTYkabiMVM.

Strauss-Schulson, Todd, dir. *Isn't It Romantic*. Broken Road, Little Engine Productions, 2019.

Strings, Sabrina. *Fearing the Black Body*: The Racial Origins of Fat Phobia. New York: NYU Press, 2019.

Wang, Wayne, dir. *Last Holiday*. Paramount Pictures, 2006.

Yandoli, Krystie Lee. "Jillian Michaels Criticized for Body-Shaming Lizzo." BuzzFeed News, January 8, 2020, https://www .buzzfeednews.com/article/krystieyandoli/jillian-michaels-lizzo -body-comments.

She's a Freak

to consider

Bellis, Nigel, and Astral Finnie, dir. *Surviving R. Kelly*. Bunim-Murray Productions, 2019.

Bergdorf, Munroe. "Photo of Munroe." Instagram, May 1, 2020, https://www.instagram.com/p/B_pklFDANSD/.

Cardi B. "WAP" (feat. Megan Thee Stallion). Atlantic Records, 2020.

The Carters. "Black Effect." *Everything Is Love*. 2018.

Contributors. "Foxy Brown (Rapper)." Wikipedia. Wikimedia Foundation, Inc., August 24, 2003. https://en.wikipedia.org/wiki /Foxy_Brown_(rapper).

———. "Lil' Kim." Wikipedia. Wikimedia Foundation, Inc., January 11, 2003. https://en.wikipedia.org/wiki/Lil%27_Kim.

Davis, Betty, "He Was a Big Freak." *They Say I'm Different*. Just Sunshine, 1974. You can listen on YouTube, https://www.youtube .com/watch?v=0eLgZvOtzy0.

djvlad. *Boosie's Biggest VladTV Interview (Full Interview)*. You-Tube, July 20, 2020, https://www.youtube.com/watch?v=l-p6C0Bpins.

Kucserka, Sarah, and Veronica West, creators. *High Fidelity*. 2020.

Pilgrim, David. "The Jezebel Stereotype." Jim Crow Museum of Racist Memorabilia, Ferris State University, https://www.ferris .edu/HTMLS/news/jimcrow/jezebel/index.htm.

Plank, Liz (@feministabulous). "'If R. Kelly Was Preying upon Young White Girls They Would Have Built a Prison on Top of Him' @rgay." Twitter, February 22, 2019, 5:25 a.m. https://twitter .com/feministabulous/status/1098997180289945602.

Rees, Dee, dir. *Pariah*. Northstar, Pariah Films, 2011.

Salt-N-Pepa. https://www.saltnpepa.com/.

Smith, Bessie. *Need a Little Sugar in My Bowl*. Columbia Records, 1931; rerelease *The Essential Bessie Smith*, Sony Legacy, 1996.

Spielberg, Steven, dir. *The Color Purple*. Warner Brothers, Guber-Peters Company, Amblin Entertainment, 1986.

Stoeffel, Kat. "Bell Hooks Was Bored by 'Anaconda.'" The Cut,

October 9, 2014, https://www.thecut.com/2014/10/bell-hooks -was-bored-by-anaconda.html.

Walker, Alice. *The Color Purple*. New York: Penguin Books, re-print ed., 2019.

Weems, Carrie Mae. "Portrait of a Woman Who Has Fallen From Grace." Photograph. 1988.

Young, Damon. "Hotep, Explained." The Root, March 5, 2016, https://www.theroot.com/hotep-explained-1790854506.

Zane. "About the Author." Simon & Schuster, https://www .simonandschuster.com/authors/Zane/269527.

Man, This Shit Is Draining
to consider

Blay, Zeba. "Amy Cooper Knew Exactly What She Was Do-ing." *HuffPost*, May 26, 2020, https://www.huffpost.com /entry/amy-cooper-knew-exactly-what-she-was-doing_n _5ecd1d89c5b6c1f281e0fbc5.

Cooper, Brittney. *Eloquent Rage*. New York: St. Martin's Press, 2018.

Correll, Charles J., and Freeman F. Gosden, creators. *The Amos 'n' Andy Show*. 1951–1955.

Fang, Marina. "*Herald Sun* Cartoonist Defends Racist, Sex-ist Serena Williams Cartoon." *HuffPost*, September 10, 2018, https://www.huffpost.com/entry/herald-sun-serena-williams -cartoon_n_5b9663ffe4b0511db3e460f0.

Gonzales, Erica. "Serena Williams Started Therapy After U.S. Open Sexism Controversy." *Harper's BAZAAR*, July 9, 2019, www.harpersbazaar.com/celebrity/latest/a28329351/serena-willi ams-therapy-us-open-sexism/.

Lorde, Audre. *Sister Outsider*. New York: Penguin Books, 2019.

Solange, featuring Lil Wayne. "Mad." *A Seat at the Table*, R8DIO, David Longstreth, Sir Dylan, Solange, Raphael Saadiq, September 30, 2016.

Extra Black
to consider

Borowitz, Andy, and Susan Borowitz, creators. *The Fresh Prince of Bel-Air*. 1990–1996.

Brooker, Charlie, creator. *Black Mirror*. 2011–2019.

Gordon, Tina, dir. *Little*. Universal Pictures, 2019.

Green, Misha, creator. *Lovecraft Country*. 2020–.

Hudlin, Reginald, dir. *Boomerang*. Paramount Pictures International, Paramount Pictures, Eddie Murphy Productions, Imagine Entertainment, 1992.

Jenkins, Barry, dir. *If Beale Street Could Talk*. Annapurna Pictures, 2018.

Kohan, Jenji, creator. *Orange Is the New Black*. 2013–2019.

Marshall, Penny, dir. *Jumpin' Jack Flash*. Lawrence Gordon Productions, Twentieth Century Fox, Silver Pictures, 1986.

McClinton, Dream. "Why Dark-Skinned Black Girls Like Me Aren't Getting Married." *The Guardian*, April 8, 2019, www.theguardian.com/lifeandstyle/2019/apr/08/dark-skinned-black-girls-dont-get-married.

McPherson & Oliver (attributed). "The Scourged Back." Photograph. April 1863.

McQueen, Steve, dir. *12 Years a Slave*. River Road, New Regency Pictures, Plan B Entertainment, 2013–2019.

Obie, Brooke. "'Lovecraft Country' Showrunner Misha Green on the Season One Finale and Growing Through Critique."

Shondaland, October 20, 2020, https://www.shondaland.com /inspire/a34418712/misha-green-lovecraft-country-finale/.

Peele, Jordan, dir. *Us*. Monkeypaw Productions, 2019.

Samuels, Allison. "A Whole Lotta Lil' Kim." *Newsweek*, Newsweek, March 14, 2010, www.newsweek.com/whole-lotta-lil-kim-160903.

Sidney, George, dir. *Show Boat*. Metro Goldwyn Mayer, Loew's Inc., 1951.

Singer, Bryan, dir. *X-Men: Apocalypse*. Bad Hat Harry, Donners' Company, Kinberg Genre, 2016.

Testa, Jessica. "The Black Photographer Making History at *Vanity Fair*." *New York Times*, July 14, 2020, https://www.nytimes .com/2020/07/14/style/the-black-photographer-making-history -at-vanity-fair.html.

Wolf, Dick, creator. *Law & Order*. 1990–2010.

Women in the World. "WITW L.A. Salon: Viola Davis on Being Told She's 'a Black Meryl Streep.'" YouTube, February 14, 2018, https://www.youtube.com/watch?v=Sf0kDGVkVzQ.

Zucker, Jerry, dir. *Ghost*. Paramount Pictures, 1990.

#CardiBIsSoProblematic

to consider

Cardi B. "Bodak Yellow." *Invasion of Privacy*. Atlantic Records, 2017.

———, *Invasion of Privacy*. Atlantic Records, 2018.

"Cardi B and Nicki Minaj Feud Turns Physical at New York Party." BBC News, September 8, 2018, http://www.bbc.com /news/entertainment-arts-45457932.

"Cardi B Is First Female Rapper to Get Two Billboard Number Ones." BBC News, July 3, 2018, http://www.bbc.com/news /newsbeat-44694302.

Coleman, Zendaya. "Cardi B Opens Up to Zendaya in the New Issue of *CR Fashion Book*." CR Fashion Book, January 10, 2019, www.crfashionbook.com/celebrity/a15956294/card-b-zendaya -cr-fashion-book-interview/.

Gardner, Chris. "Cardi B Unleashes Expletive-Filled Rant over 'Access Hollywood' Interview." *Billboard*, October 4, 2019, https://www.billboard.com/index.php/articles/news/8532223 /cardi-b-rant-access-hollywood-interview.

Golshan, Tara, and Emily Stewart. "Cardi B and Bernie Sanders's Video, and Her Longstanding Interest in Politics, Explained." Vox, August 15, 2019, https://www.vox.com/2019/8/15 /20805989/cardi-b-bernie-sanders-watch-video-2020-nail-salon.

Migos. "MotorSport" (feat. Nicki Minaj and Cardi B). *Culture II*. Quality Control Music, 2017.

Minaj, Nicki. *Queen Radio with Nicki Minaj*. Queen Radio. Beats 1, August 2018, https://music.apple.com/us/curator/queen-radio /1391364917.

Penrose, Nerisha. "A Timeline of Nicki Minaj & Cardi B's Complicated Relationship." *Billboard*, November 1, 2017, https://www .billboard.com/articles/columns/hip-hop/8022232/nicki-minaj -cardi-b-timeline-motorsport.

Perry, Katy. "Swish Swish" (feat. Nicki Minaj). *Witness*. Capitol Records, 2017.

Remy Ma. "Shether." Empire Distribution, 2017, https://www .youtube.com/watch?v=FcouOGFhZ9I

Girlhood

to consider

Atchison, Doug, dir. *Akeelah and the Bee*. Out of the Blue . . . Entertainment, 2006.

Blay, Zeba. "'Girlhood' Is Now Streaming on Netflix. We Spoke to the Director About Race, Gender & the Universality of the Story." *Shadow and Act*, May 19, 2015, shadowandact.com /girlhood-is-now-streaming-on-netflix-we-spoke-to-the-director -about-race-gender-the-universality-of-the-story.

———, "White Critics Love 'Three Billboards' Like They Love Their Racist Uncles." *HuffPost*, December 15, 2017, https://www .huffpost.com/entry/white-critics-three-billboards-racism_n _5a3135eae4b091ca268479f3.

Campbell, Hayley. "'The World Is Infested with Evil!' When Kathy Acker Met the Spice Girls." *The Guardian*, February 28, 2018, www.theguardian.com/music/2018/feb/26/when-kathy-acker-met -the-spice-girls.

Communication and Marketing Staff. "Report Critiques Inclusion Among Film Critics." USC Annenberg School for Communication and Journalism, June 11, 2018, https://annenberg.usc .edu/news/research/report-critiques-inclusion-among-film-critics.

Daniels, Lee, dir. *Precious*. Smokewood Entertainment Group, 2009.

Eckert, Maddi. "Civil Rights Leader Angela Davis Speaks at Bovard." *Daily Trojan*, February 24, 2015, https://dailytrojan.com /2015/02/23/civil-rights-leader-angela-davis-speaks-at-bovard/.

Erbland, Kate. "Female Film Critics Are Still the Minority, and New Study Finds They're Predominantly Covering Movies About Women." IndieWire, August 6, 2018, https://www.indiewire.com /2018/07/female-film-critics-minority-new-study-1201984259/.

Fanon, Frantz. *Black Skin, White Masks*. New York: Grove Press, 1967.

Farah, Safy-Hallan. "All Alone in Their White Girl Pain." Hip to Waste, August 1, 2020, https://hiptowaste.substack.com/p/all -alone-in-their-white-girl-pain.

Fleck, Ryan, dir. *Half Nelson*. Journeyman Pictures, 2006.

Gunn, Bill, dir. *Ganja & Hess*. Kelly/Jordan Enterprises, 1973.

Harris, Leslie, dir. *Just Another Girl on the I.R.T.* Miramax, 1992.

Hope, Hannah. "Mel B Reveals She Was Bombarded with Racist Hate Mail When She Bought a House in Buckinghamshire." *The Sun*, June 14, 2020, www.thesun.co.uk/tvandshowbiz/11859094 /mel-b-racisit-hate-mail-buckinghamshire-village/.

Iscove, Robert, dir. *She's All That.* Miramax Films, Film Colony, 1999.

Jay-Z and Kanye West. "Niggas in Paris." *Watch the Throne.* Roc-A-Fella Records, Roc Nation, and Def Jam Recordings, 2011.

Junger, Gil, dir. *10 Things I Hate About You.* Touchstone Pictures, Mad Chance, 1999.

Ledbetter, Les. "15,000 EXHORTED BY ANGELA DAVIS." *New York Times,* June 30, 1972, https://www.nytimes.com/1972 /06/30/archives/5000-exhorted-by-angela-davis-garden-crowd -hears-plea-for-socialist.html.

Lee, Spike, dir. *25th Hour.* 40 Acres and a Mule, 2003.

———, dir. *Bamboozled.* 40 Acres and a Mule, 2000.

———, dir. *Crooklyn.* 40 Acres and a Mule, 1994.

———, dir. Da *Sweet Bloood of Jesus.* 40 Acres and a Mule, 2014.

———, dir. *Do the Right Thing.* 40 Acres and a Mule, 1989.

———, dir. *She's Gotta Have It.* 40 Acres and a Mule, 1986.

Lemmons, Kasi, dir. *Eve's Bayou.* ChubbCo Film, 1997.

Mahoney, Victoria, dir. *Yelling to the Sky.* Chicken and Egg Pictures, YTTS LLC, 2011.

Morrison, Toni. *Playing in the Dark.* Cambridge: Harvard University Press, 1992.

Omawale, Tchaiko, dir. *Solace.* Big Vision Empty Wallet, 2019.

Poe, Tayarisha, dir. *Selah and the Spades*. Argent Pictures,2020.

"Raw Footage: Texas Cop Draws Gun on Pool-Party Teens." Posted to the *Wall Street Journal* YouTube channel, June 8, 2015, https://www.youtube.com/watch?v=z6tTfoifB7Q.

Reed, Peyton, dir. *Bring It On*. Beacon Pictures, 2000.

Rees, Dee, dir. *Pariah*. Northstar, Pariah Films, 2011.

Rihanna. "Diamonds." *Unapologetic*. Def Jam Recordings and SRP Records, 2012.

Sciamma, Céline, dir. *Girlhood*. Hold Up Films, 2014.

——, dir. *Portrait of a Lady on Fire*. Lilies Films, 2019.

Sehgal, Parul. "A Mother and Son, Fleeing for Their Lives over Treacherous Terrain." *New York Times*, January 17, 2020, https://www.nytimes.com/2020/01/17/books/review-american-dirt-jeanine-cummins.html.

"This Video from 1997 of the Spice Girls on Dutch TV Calling Out Blackface Is Perfect." *The Independent*. March 11, 2017, https://www.independent.co.uk/arts-entertainment/music/news/spice-girls-blackface-video-dutch-tv-presenter-black-pete-tradition-racist-a7624176.html.

Tillman, Jr., George, dir. *The Hate U Give*. Fox 2000 Pictures, Temple Hill Entertainment, State Street Pictures, 2018.

Zeitlin, Benh, dir. *Beasts of the Southern Wild*. Court 13 Pictures, 2012.

Strong Black Lead

to consider

ACLU of Washington. "Timeline of the Muslim Ban," May 23, 2017, https://www.aclu-wa.org/pages/timeline-muslim-ban.

Akil, Mara Brock. *Being Mary Jane*. Akil Productions, 2013–.

Brinlee, Morgan. "More Black Women Are Killed In America Than Any Other Race, a New CDC Report Says." *Bustle*, July 22, 2017, https://www.bustle.com/p/more-black-women-are-killed-in-america-than-any-other-race-a-new-cdc-report-says-71955.

Burnett-Zeigler, Inger E. "Opinion: Young Black People Are Killing Themselves." *New York Times,* December 16, 2019, https://www.nytimes.com/2019/12/16/opinion/young-black-people-suicide.html.

CDC. "Mental and Behavioral Health—African Americans." U.S. Department of Health and Human Services Office of Minority Services. Accessed January 15, 2021, https://minorityhealth.hhs.gov/omh/browse.aspx?lvl=4&lvlid=24.

Contributors. "Killing of Eric Garner." Wikipedia. Wikimedia Foundation, Inc., July 19, 2014, https://en.wikipedia.org/wiki/Killing_of_Eric_Garner.

———. "Shooting of Michael Brown." Wikipedia. Wikimedia Foundation, Inc., August 11, 2014, https://en.wikipedia.org/wiki/Shooting_of_Michael_Brown.

———. "Shooting of Oscar Grant." Wikipedia. Wikimedia Foundation, Inc., January 6, 2009, https://en.wikipedia.org/wiki/Shooting_of_Oscar_Grant.

———. "Shooting of Philando Castile." Wikipedia. Wikimedia Foundation, Inc., July 7, 2016, https://en.wikipedia.org/wiki/Shooting_of_Philando_Castile.

———. "Stoneman Douglas High School Shooting." Wikipedia. Wikimedia Foundation, Inc., February 14, 2018, https://en.wikipedia.org/wiki/Stoneman_Douglas_High_School_shooting.

Coogler, Ryan, dir. *Black Panther.* Marvel Studios, Walt Disney Studios Motion Pictures, 2019.

Darabont, Frank, and Angela Kang, creators. *The Walking Dead.* AMC Studios, 2010.

Ewing, Eve. "Eve L. Ewing." Twitter. Accessed January 15, 2021, https://twitter.com/eveewing.

Hill, Jack, dir. *Coffy*. American International Pictures (AIP), 1973.

Human Rights Campaign. "Violence Against the Transgender Community in 2019." Accessed January 15, 2021, https://www.hrc.org/resources/violence-against-the-transgender-community-in-2019.

Lee, Spike, creator. *She's Gotta Have It*. 40 Acres and a Mule Filmworks, Netflix, 2017–2019.

Levinson, Sam, creator. *Euphoria*. A24, Home Box Office (HBO), 2019–.

Rae, Issa, and Larry Wilmore, creators. *Insecure*. 3 Arts Entertainment, 2016–.

Ray, Michael. "Orlando Shooting of 2016." *Encyclopædia Britannica*. Accessed January 15, 2021, https://www.britannica.com/event/Orlando-shooting-of-2016.

Rhimes, Shonda, creator. *Scandal*. Shondaland, 2012–2018.

St. Félix, Doreen. "The Very American Killing of Nia Wilson." *New Yorker*, July 31, 2018, https://www.newyorker.com/culture/cultural-comment/the-very-american-killing-of-nia-wilson.

Tate Taylor, dir. *The Help*. 1492 Pictures, Harbinger Pictures, 2011.

Free of Cares

to consider

"Biography." Josephine Baker: The Official Site of Josephine Baker, https://www.cmgww.com/stars/baker/about/biography/. Accessed January 17, 2021.

Bowman, John, Topper Carew, and Martin Lawrence, creators. *Martin*. 1992–1997.

Burns, Ken, dir. *The Civil War*. American Documentaries Inc., 1990.

"Carefree Black Girl" pennant. Rayo & Honey, https://rayoandhoney.com/collections/pennants/products/carefree-black-girl.

Combahee River Collective. "The Combahee River Collective Statement." 1977. Available on Blackpast.com, https://www.blackpast.org/african-american-history/combahee-river-collective-statement-1977/.

Contributors. "Carefree Black Girls." Wikipedia. Wikimedia Foundation, Inc., September 3, 2016, https://en.wikipedia.org/wiki/Carefree_Black_Girls.

DiBiase, Kevin (@Hylianhero777). "'Arrest the Cops Who Killed Breonna Taylor' Becoming a Meme." Twitter, June 21, 2020, 12:14 p.m., https://twitter.com/Hylianhero777/status/1274858294654504960.

Hairston, Tahirah. "Cree Summer on the Myth of the Carefree Black Girl." Fusion, August 25, 2016, https://fusion.tv/story/339815/cree-summer-diversity-animation-carefree-black-girl/?utm_source=twitter&utm_medium=social&utm_campaign=socialshare&utm_content=theme_bottom_mobile.

Hawkins, Danielle. "Carefree Black Girls." Tumblr, https://carefreeblackgirls.tumblr.com/. (Note: Tumblr page currently blocked.)

Heisel, Andrew. "The Rise and Fall of an All-American Catchphrase: 'Free, White, and 21.'" Jezebel, September 10, 2015, https://theattic.jezebel.com/the-rise-and-fall-of-an-all-american-catchphrase-free-1729621311.

Ibrahim, Shamira. "Why I'm over the 'Carefree Black Girl' Label." The Root, March 11, 2016, https://www.theroot.com/why-i-m-over-the-carefree-black-girl-label-1790854569.

LEGENDS, TV. "Debbie Allen Discusses Why Lisa Bonet Left

'A Different World' - EMMYTVLEGENDS.ORG." *YouTube*, You-Tube, July 30 2015, www.youtube.com/watch?v=-yPzsKSzcaQ.

Noble, Safiya Umoja. *Algorithms of Oppression*: How Search Engines Reinforce Racism. New York: NYU Press, 2018.

"Quanna." http://www.quannathemc.com/.

Romano, Aja. "World War 3 Memes as Therapy: Coping with War and Crisis Through Memes." Vox, January 17, 2020, https://www.vox.com/2020/1/17/21065113/world-war-3-memes-iran-2020-saleem-alhabash-interview.

Taylor, Breonna (@PrettyN_Paidd). Twitter, https://twitter.com/PrettyN_Paidd.

Weekes, Princess. "Bill Cosby's Treatment of Lisa Bonet Was a Sign." The Mary Sue, March 9, 2018, https://www.themarysue.com/bill-cosbys-lisa-bonet/.